THE COMPLETE
surfaces and finishes
DIRECTORY

THE COMPLETE
surfaces and finishes
DIRECTORY

paint ■ plaster ■ wallpaper ■ tile ■ wood ■ metal ■ glass

EMMA SCATTERGOOD

WATSON-GUPTILL
PUBLICATIONS

New York

Design and text copyright © The Ivy Press Limited 2001

First published in the United states in 2001
by Watson-Guptill Publications, a division of
BPI Communications, Inc., 770 Broadway,
New York, NY 10003.

Library of Congress Catalog Card Number: 2001087331

ISBN 0-8230-5030-0

This book was conceived, designed, and
produced by
THE IVY PRESS LIMITED
The Old Candlemakers, West Street
Lewes, East Sussex BN7 1UP

Creative Director: PETER BRIDGEWATER
Publisher: SOPHIE COLLINS
Art Director: CLARE BARBER
Design: BLUE BANANA ASSOCIATES
Editorial Director: STEVE LUCK
Senior Project Editor: APRIL McCROSKIE
Editor: LINDSAY McTEAGUE
Set and Furniture Painting: PAUL ALLEN
Studio Photography: CALVEY TAYLOR-HAW
Picture Researcher: LIZ EDDISON
Printed in China by
Winner Print and Packaging
This book is typeset in 9/16 Gill Sans Light

1 2 3 4 5 6 7 8 9 /08 07 06 05 04 03 02 01 00

contents

introduction

Something wonderful has happened to interior design over the past ten years, and especially in the last five: It has become fun.

Prior to that time it always seemed that "design" was something that only the wealthy could indulge in, and, despite the efforts of style gurus such as Terence Conran, it was not something the average householder became involved in. Home improvement yes, but not design. Then the change began.

During the 1980s middle-market homes magazine titles appeared, and soon multiplied, and then the big break came when television became involved. Soon TV slots for interior design advice rose from the ranks of daytime television to peak viewing times, turning a host of hitherto unknown designers into household names and in turn producing new ranges of paints and wallpapers.

Now everyone wants to have a home that looks

Dining areas can look equally as effective in bright, harmonizing colors as they do in pale, neutral tones.

fantastic, whether it is a one-bedroom apartment or a five-bedroom colonial—and they can. All it needs is a little confidence and some good advice, which is where this book comes in.

Often, in the name of good television, practicality, quality, and durability are sidelined—which is fine when a room is on view for five minutes, but not so good if you have to live with the decor for any length of time. This book takes the approach that, if you are going to invest in your home, then you want to invest in something that is going to not only

Plain cream is the ultimate in elegant simplicity. The painting adds a focal feature to this dining room.

This alcove has been painted in a complementary contrasting color and offset by a chair in a similar tone to the surrounding walls, creating a balanced look.

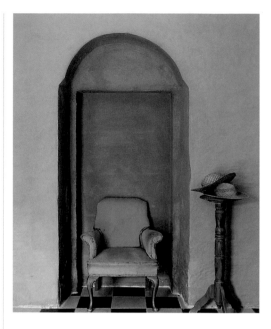

Although this modern bathroom is decorated in cool blue colors, the end result is not too cold.

look good, but also remain stylish. The book includes plenty of hot fashion ideas for the home to inspire you, but they are backed up by practical advice on each surface's durability and suitability for your home, and includes maintenance tips to keep it looking good. Each chapter also features an easy-to-follow Applications Chart so you can see at a glance whether a particular material will work in a specific way.

We are surrounded by different surfaces to decorate and finish —from the ceilings and walls, to the worktops, woodwork, and floors. The way in which you approach those surfaces will dictate the style and success of your finished room. This book will help you choose the right look for each room. It doesn't assume any prior knowledge of do it yourself, and gives answers to the common questions that many people are too nervous to ask in a DIY (do it your-self) store, such as "What is the difference between an oil-based and a water-based paint?" or "What sort of tiles can I put on the floor?"

The book is divided into eight sections, tabbed for ease of use. The first seven sections look individ-ually at paint, paint finishes, plaster, wallpaper, tiles, wood, metal, and glass. The final section looks at individual rooms around the home, offering advice and providing inspiration for how to achieve the look you want.

Each chapter also features two projects for you to try at home, with step-by-step instructions to help you to achieve a professional look. There are projects on how to achieve special paint effects and create different finishes with plaster; how to make a mosaic-framed mirror and tile a floor with a pat-terned border; how to paint a wooden floor to give it a fresh, modern look; how to make a metal front to transform the look of a plain cupboard door; and how to etch a glass window to decorate it and add privacy.

In order to inspire extra confidence in putting together a color scheme, there is plenty of advice on color theory, including a color wheel and expla-nations concerning the differences between

The plain-colored walls are the perfect backdrop to this elaborate bed.

so-called warm and cool colors. There are even suggestions on which colors will work especially well together—and where in the home. There are tips throughout to give you extra hints on how to achieve the perfect end result. At the end of each chapter, there are further suggestions on how you can combine each surface with other materials in a room to create exactly the look you are after.

Designing and decorating your home can be a daunting task, but this book aims to make the decision process easier and, hopefully, prevent you from making any costly mistakes. Good luck, and have fun.

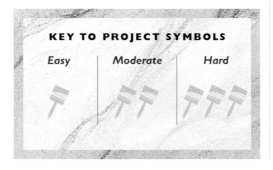

KEY TO PROJECT SYMBOLS

Easy	Moderate	Hard

Invest in some good quality tools to ensure more professional results.

simple
paint

THERE is one finish that can do more than change the look of a room, it can change the whole mood. Paint allows you to be creative and even adventurous. The range of colors is almost infinite— and even an amateur at DIY can experiment with clever touches such as painting one wall in a room a different color. Soon you will find your confidence growing and will be using paint to transform furniture, tiles, and even floors.

basics

UNDERSTANDING PAINT

Cast your eye along the shelves in any home improvement store and you will find a confusingly wide range of paint types. Here then, succinctly, is the lowdown on the different paints, what they are, and how they can work for you.

Any paint is made up of pigment (to give it color), binders (to make it adhere to a surface), and a solution of water or spirit, depending on whether it is a latex or oil paint. It will also contain chemicals to speed up the drying process, and perhaps extenders to make it go further.

The color you choose for your walls and ceiling will determine the style and mood of a room.

For painting an interior you need to understand the difference between oil-based and latex, or water-based, paints (see also pp. 14–17). Basically, oil paint has a high resin content and, when dry, is very hard-wearing and glossy, making it the perfect covering for surfaces—such as wood and metal —that need extra protection from knocks and water. Latex matte paint dries to a more matte finish, is cheaper than oil paint, and so is more suited to walls and ceilings.

PRIMERS AND SEALERS

Some surfaces need to be primed or sealed before painting to achieve a better finish and make the paint cover a greater area. Primers give a rougher surface for the paint to adhere to, making it easier to cover materials such as MDF, wood, and sheetrock; sealers add an impermeable layer to the surface (of plaster or wood, for example) to stop it 'leaking' on to your new paint finish. There are various types of primer and sealer, so it's best to take advice from a decorating store salesperson and then to follow the manufacturer's recommendations on the label.

wall roller

brush

small roller

TIPS FOR A PERFECT FINISH

Invest in good quality brushes. They will not shed so many hairs on to your handiwork and will last longer if you look after them.

If you are covering a large area use a roller for speed. A medium pile sleeve is best for water-based paints and a short pile one for oil paints. Radiator rollers have a small diameter to allow them to slip behind the radiator, saving you from having to lift it off the wall.

Investing in good painting tools will help you create a professional finish.

Try to paint in natural light whenever possible. Sometimes artificial light can make it difficult to see whether you have covered the wall evenly.

If you have to interrupt your painting until the following day, save yourself the bother of washing rollers and brushes by wrapping them in saran wrap and keeping them in the refrigerator.

MAINTENANCE

Surfaces painted with matte latex paints need to be cleaned with caution as the paint may rub off. You can normally remove marks from small areas, such as around door handles and light switches, with a mild cleanser. Special-purpose bathroom and kitchen paints are a little more robust, and oil-based paints such as gloss and satinwood can be cleaned easily with a damp cloth and some mild detergent.

oil-based paints

Oil-based paints are ideal for woodwork, such as window frames, baseboards, and even floorboards.

Kitchen units can be given a fresh new look with a coat of satinwood or gloss paint.

With their diverse spectrum of colors and such a variety of compositions that they can be applied to a wide range of materials, oil-based paints are now more exciting than ever. Usually, because of their high resin content and tough shiny finish, they are still largely used for the woodwork around the home—baseboards, window frames, and doors —but they can be used on tiles and melamine too. The age of the ubiquitous brilliant white baseboard and door has long gone, however. Rather than being overshadowed by the walls, today's woodwork has an edge and vitality of its own. The new colors allow you to create vibrant contrasts with the surrounding paintwork or to choose a more subtle variation of its tone.

gloss paint

There are several different types of oil-based paint, each designed for a particular application or finish. All of these paints have a spirit base, so they are not soluble with water, which means you will need to clean your brushes with turpentine instead.

■ **LIQUID GLOSS** Most often used on wood and metal, it requires an undercoat. Coverage is about 45yd²/gal (17m²/liter).

■ **SATINWOOD** With a less shiny, more subtle finish than gloss, it is good for woodwork and does not require an undercoat. Coverage is around 45yd²/gal (17m²/liter).

■ **NON-DRIP GLOSS** This has a sticky, gel-like texture so it does not run (useful for painting doors). It doesn't require an undercoat, but you should still prime bare wood before using it. Coverage is around 32–41yd²/gal (12–15m²/liter).

■ **SELF-UNDERCOATING GLOSS** This covers most surfaces with a single coat, but is creamier than non-drip gloss. Coverage is around 27yd²/gal (10m²/liter).

■ **MID-SHEEN OIL-BASED PAINT** Also known as eggshell. It offers an even less glossy finish than satinwood, but is less resistant and harder to keep clean. You will normally need to apply two coats, but it doesn't require an undercoat. Coverage is around 43yd²/gal (16m²/liter).

Some paint manufacturers can mix up the same color in both latex and oil-based paint, allowing you to continue the same color from your walls onto your woodwork.

gloss paint

latex paints

From shades of white or cool blue to burnt orange or deepest chocolate, latex, or water-based, paint can transform a room in a matter of minutes. Of all the surface finishes, this is the easiest and most fun to experiment with. The big paint manufacturers now produce a better range of colors available off the shelf than ever before, but if you are keen to paint your bedroom walls in exactly the shade of your favorite lipstick, you can do so. Just take a sample to a large design center store to be color matched by computer and then see the paint mixed on the spot for you. Always buy a little more than you think you will need and get it all mixed at the same time to avoid any slight variation in the mixing and so in the final color.

Warm red walls make an ideal color for a dining area. Red is thought to stimulate the appetite, and the cozy atmosphere encourages diners to linger.

Your choice of finish comes down to aesthetics and practicality. If you are not too worried about whether or not you can clean the surface easily, you

have a free rein to go for as matte or silky a finish as you require. Flat matte finishes look best in period properties, where an honest aged look is called for. Many companies now produce a special range of traditional colors with such a flat finish, based on the colors used in restored historical homes. Silkier finishes suit more modern rooms and are more practical when it comes to cleaning.

■ **VINYL MATTE LATEX** This does not require an undercoat and is the most popular choice for walls and ceilings, giving a flat matte finish that will hide many of a wall's imperfections. Coverage is around 39–41yd²/gal (14–15m²/liter).

■ **VINYL SILK LATEX** This has a silky finish, which makes it ideal for walls that might need cleaning (such as in children's rooms), but it also shows up any imperfections in the wall surface more readily. It does not require an undercoat and coverage is roughly 36–39yd²/gal (13–14m²/liter).

■ **SOLID LATEX** Available in matte or silk finish, this paint comes in a paint tray, ready to apply with a roller. It is useful for painting ceilings as its thicker texture reduces drips. Coverage is about 32yd²/gal (12m²/liter).

Be aware of the view from one room to another when choosing paint colors for each space. Opt for colors that complement, rather than clash with, each other.

latex

dragging brush

special-purpose paints

Thanks to the plethora of interior design programs on TV, we have all been encouraged to be more adventurous with paint. This in turn has triggered the creation of special-purpose paints to make transforming our homes easier. There are paints to cover a multitude of sins—from melamine kitchen units to avocado bathroom tiles—as well as those that are a fashion statement in themselves.

Glamor has entered the world of interior design. Back in the late 1980s, few people would have dreamt of adding glitter to a wall, but at the start of the 21st century, there is a craze for all things shiny and space age, and the special latex paints on the shelves are proof. For those who are less ostentatious, the trend for neutral, earthy shades and texture has resulted in paints that look

Paints designed specifically for painting floors offer extra durability in just one coat.

good enough to touch. With a can of paint, a suede effect, or even a denim look, can be achieved at the stroke of a brush. The choice is almost infinite.

Here is a selection of the more practical special-purpose paints:

■ **ANTI-CONDENSATION PAINT** Useful for steamy areas, this paint is moisture resistant.

■ **TILE PAINT** Use on top of two coats of tile primer to cover old bathroom and kitchen wall tiles.

■ **MELAMINE PAINT** Perfect for transforming old built-in units in bedrooms and kitchens. Use with a primer.

■ **FLOOR PAINT** This can be used on boards, concrete, stone, or brick for a hard-wearing gloss finish. (It takes 16 hours to dry.)

■ **FINISHES AND GLAZES** These will help you achieve anything from a suede effect to a rag-rolled look on walls and woodwork—you just brush them on.

Stencils and stamps are great for brightening up children's rooms. You can use latex paint, but all kinds of paints designed specially for stenciling and stamping are available in small pots.

floor paint

warm colors

Choosing your paint colors can be even more fun and rewarding if you are aware that the world of color can be divided into two halves—warm and cool. Turn to the color wheel on page 24 and you will see immediately how it can be split: one half of warmer colors, the red/yellow side; the other half of cooler colors, the blue/green side. This is, of course, all based on people's perception of color and the psychological effect that color has on them. Color affects mood, and people have exploited this for years. Consider that dining rooms have traditionally been painted in a warm, rich red. Why? Because it looks fantastic by candlelight, and the warm feeling it creates also makes guests happier to linger at a table. And red is said to stimulate the appetite, too.

So, if your room is on the shady side of the house, for example, and receives a cold light, paint it

warm colors

Warm colors of terracotta and pink painted on the walls create a cozy, intimate space which looks great by sunlight, artificial light, or candlelight and is perfect for bedrooms.

with sunny shades of orange, red, and gold. You will feel how much cozier it becomes. Warm colors can create a snug living room, an intimate bedroom, or a more welcoming hallway.

You can use also warm paint colors to balance a room's imperfections, making its dimensions appear more regular. Warm colors have the effect of appearing to advance toward you, so if a room is long and thin, try painting the walls at the ends in a warmer color than those at the sides to make them seem to move inwards. If a ceiling feels too high, painting it in a warmer shade than the walls will seem to lower it.

Choose wall colors that will be complemented by the furniture in the room.

Earthy tones, such as sand, terracotta, and muted greens, complement each other, producing a balanced, warm color scheme.

cool colors

cool colors

Lavender and lilac are derived from blue, and create a cool, fresh, and contemporary look, while purples with more red in them can add warmth to a color scheme.

The cool side of the color wheel is made up of blues, greens, and violets, although violet can appear warm or cool, depending on the proportion of red and blue used to mix it (a blue violet looks cool, but one with more of a red base appears warm).

Generally people are more concerned about adding warmth to a room than achieving the opposite effect, but don't ignore the green and blue side of the wheel as these colors can create beautifully elegant, relaxing interiors. The association with the colors of sea, sky, and nature helps to give shades of blue and green the power to soothe, which could explain why they are often used in hospitals, and why green is a popular choice for a study, too.

Recently the fresh palette of mint—even lime—green and violet has become fashionable once

more, and these combinations have appeared in every room in the modern home, from the bathroom to the kitchen and living room. Cool colors work well in most settings—as long as the light a room receives is warm enough to balance them. If your room does not get much natural light, opt for warmer tones, but if it is bathed in sunlight for most of the day, you can experiment with cool pastels and still create a welcoming room.

Green is a very calming color and works well in areas that see a lot of human traffic, such as hallways.

Cool mint greens, aqua, and Wedgwood blue help create a sense of space and airiness, and work well in modern and traditional homes.

Use the fact that cool colors appear to recede to make a small narrow space seem larger. You can make a low ceiling appear higher, for instance, by painting it a cooler color than the walls. There are many options —surely you can be more imaginative than just choosing neutral white?

paint color combinations

If you have chosen paint as your finish, you need to use it with flair and confidence—which is where the color wheel can help. It is a useful tool for putting together paint colors successfully in any interior, since as well as being divided into warm and cool colors, the wheel can be used to suggest various color combinations.

Colors that lie on opposite sides of the color wheel are said to be complementary, or contrasting. Those on the same side are harmonious.

CONTRASTING SCHEMES

Colors that lie on opposite sides of the wheel are said to be contrasting, or complementary. Putting together a scheme with two contrasting colors, such as blue and orange, never fails to create a lively, vibrant effect, but be careful not to use both colors in equal proportions. Instead, allow one color to dominate.

HARMONIOUS SCHEMES

Colors that lie on the same side of the wheel are known as harmonious colors. Blues and greens or yellows and oranges are two popular harmonious combinations. Using harmonious cool colors will make a small room feel more spacious, while a large room will feel relaxing if finished in harmonious warm colors, such as gold and red.

SINGLE COLOR SCHEMES

If you are still nervous about mixing and matching your paint colors, why not consider a single color scheme? This does not mean using exactly the same color throughout, but using different tones of one color on walls, floor, fixtures, and furnishings.

ACCENT COLORS

All schemes will benefit from a third, accent color used sparingly in the room. It can be a harmonizing or contrasting color; the choice is yours. Experiment with samples of one of each to see how a splash of a third color affects the character of a room, often bringing it to life. Color swatches can help you match the tones.

This striking bathroom makes good use of different tones of the same color to create a harmonious look

Here the neutral walls are offset by the window blinds and the splash of color provided by the flowers.

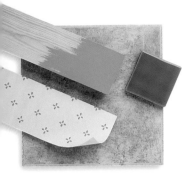

combining

The beauty of paint is its versatility and the fact that it is the perfect foil to any other finish. Choose the right color and type of paint to complement the other surfaces as well as the style or mood of the room.

Paint works well with stone, paper, and wood—just choose a shade that complements your other surfaces.

Wallpaper and painted woodwork are beautifully combined here to create a lower-wall finish that, being easier to retouch, is more practical than the luxurious wallpaper above it.

PAINT AND WALLPAPER

As a wall treatment, paint and wallpaper are a useful combination, allowing you to add pattern and perhaps another color, without committing yourself to a room papered from floor to ceiling. In a traditional style of home consider the effect of papering down to chair rail height, then painting below that. This not only adds interest to the wall but is also more practical, since you can touch up the paintwork if it gets scuffed, and keep the more costly paper out of harm's way.

A more contemporary approach to the paint and wallpaper combination is to paper or paint one entire wall to create a different, yet complementary, backdrop to one area of the room. This has come about mainly in response to the move toward more open-plan living, allowing you to define one area of a large space as, say, your dining room and to create different moods.

PAINT AND NATURAL MATERIALS

Wood, slate, and stone work well in any setting and can be combined with almost any color, although you need to consider the tone of the natural material when choosing your paint. Pine's tones work

Here the rather orange tone of pine wood has been muted by painting the wood of the stairs in a blue color that complements the woodwork elsewhere in the room.

well with golden colors, but may need a splash of a contrasting color to prevent the overall effect from being too yellow. Dark woods, such as mahogany, go well with rich reds and yellows, but take care that the finished scheme isn't too dark. Generally, matte paint finishes are more successful when combined with wood and stone than shiny gloss.

PAINT WITH GLASS AND METAL

A room dominated by glass and metal is likely to have a contemporary edge. Perhaps it is a warehouse or loft conversion, with expanses of glass and

The crisp, modern lines of this glass extension have been softened by painting the woodwork in a more traditional shade of green.

bare metal. Or maybe it is a modern kitchen, with stainless steel appliances and glass shelving. In either setting paint will work well, offering exactly the color and texture you require. For a fresh, minimalist look opt for a variation on white or, for something more exciting, choose a deep jewel shade for the walls.

brushes

A STRIPED WALL

Make your wall a work of art by striping it in a range of different shades. The effect is lively and emphasizes the height of the room. Here, we've used eight different shades of pink, ranging from a bright candy pink to a subtle soft pinkish-white. The colors are based on the same hue but vary in depth and intensity.

INGREDIENTS

- *Measuring tape*
- *Pencil*
- *Plumb line*
- *Chalk*
- *Masking tape*
- *Medium-sized brush*
- *Small brush for the edges*
- *8 small pots of vinyl latex paint, chosen in closely related shades*

METHOD

■ Start with a clean, dry surface. If it is pale and matte, there is no need for an undercoat. Measure the area of the wall you wish to paint and divide it by eight. This will give you the area to be covered by each shade, and thus the amount of paint you will need. It's likely that the smallest amount of paint you will be able to buy is 1 quart (1 liter), so there may be some left over, although many paint ranges come in smaller sample cans, which may help. As a rough guide, most paints will cover between 6–7yd^2 per pint or half liter; unless your chosen wall is vast, you are unlikely to need the full quantity.

■ Measure the full width of the wall and divide by eight. This gives you the width of each stripe. Draw small pencil marks at the top and bottom of the wall, at the edge of the first stripe. Run your chalk down the plumb line holding it close against the wall to leave a faint chalk line. Mask off the stripe with masking tape, following the chalk line. Repeat until each strip is masked off on its outer edge.

■ Choose which order you want your colors to follow and paint the first stripe with the medium brush, brushing the edges of the masking tape gently. Leave to dry, then peel off the first strip of tape and repeat the process with the second stripe. When all eight stripes are completed, and you've reached the far side of the wall, go over any smeared or uneven edges with the small brush.

eggshell paint   steel wool   eggshell paint

DISTRESSED PAINT
FINISH FOR FURNITURE

Use paint to help you create the look you want for your furniture as well as your walls. "Shabby chic" is a fashion that seems destined to be with us for some time. You can transform a plain piece straight from the store (we chose a small, inexpensive cupboard) into something that looks as if it has been loved for generations.

INGREDIENTS

- *Small wooden cupboard*
- *Fine-gauge sandpaper*
- *Paint primer*
- *Undercoat*
- *Two contrasting colors of eggshell paint*
- *Medium paintbrush*
- *Small paintbrush*
- *Fine-gauge steel wool*
- *Matte or satin varnish*

METHOD

■ If the wood of your chosen piece is bare, rub it down lightly with fine-gauge sandpaper, then paint it with a coat of primer and leave to dry. Add a thinly painted layer of undercoat. Leave overnight or until it is completely dry.

■ Apply a coat of your first color of eggshell. This is the color that you will see peeping through in the "worn" areas. Here, we used green.

■ When the base coat is dry, paint on a top coat of your second color of eggshell. Here, we used bright yellow.

■ Allow the paint to dry completely, then use the steel wool to rub off the top coat of paint in the areas that would normally become the most worn— around the handle, at the corners of the piece, and in the corners of the front panels. Work very gently—you are aiming for a subtly aged effect rather than great areas of contrasting color.

■ When you are happy with the effect, dust off the piece with a clean, dry cloth and finish with a coat of matte or satin varnish to protect the finish.

FINISH	APPLICATIONS
LIQUID GLOSS Oil-based paint	Most commonly used on wood and metal to produce a shiny, hard finish that will withstand water and gentle cleaning products. It requires an undercoat.
SATINWOOD Oil-based paint	A less shiny, more subtle finish than gloss, Satinwood is good for woodwork such as mantelpieces, interior baseboards, and window sills. It doesn't require an undercoat.
EGGSHELL Mid sheen oil-based paint	Good for period properties in which a shiny gloss-paint finish would look too "new." Eggshell gives a less glossy finish than satinwood, but is less tough and is harder to keep clean. Normally you will need to apply two coats, but it doesn't require an undercoat.
VINYL MATTE LATEX Water-based paint	The most popular choice for walls and ceilings, giving a flat matte finish which can hide many imperfections that a wall may have. The choice of colors available is almost infinite. You can pick ready-mixed colors off the shelf (generally the fashionable colors and "safer" shades) or some manufacturers provide paint-mixing machines within decorating stores to offer a wider choice of shades and colors.
VINYL SILK LATEX Water-based paint	The silky finish makes it suitable for walls that need regular cleaning such as those in kitchens, bathrooms, hallways, and children's rooms. It helps to reflect light more than a matte surface, but this means it also shows up any imperfections in the wall surface more readily.

FINISH	APPLICATIONS
TILE PAINT To change the color of kitchen and bathroom tiles	Use on top of two coats of tile primer to cover up old bathroom and kitchen wall tiles. This is a good, economical way of transforming a room, but the surface will not last very long in areas where the tiles suffer a lot of wear and tear, such as shower stalls. If the tiles have a raised pattern this will still show through the new color.
FLOOR PAINT An oil-based heavy duty paint	This can be used on floorboards, concrete, stone, or brick to give a hardwearing gloss finish that looks great in modern or informal country-style interiors. At the moment the color range is quite limited, but classic white and black are the obvious favorites. It takes 16 hours to dry.
PRIMER A preparatory covering of paint	Primer is painted onto a surface such as bare wood, metal, or plaster to reduce its absorbency. This means when you then paint the surface with your chosen finishing paint, less paint needs to be applied, thus saving both time and money. It is possible to make your own primer by thinning the chosen finishing paint with water or paint thinner (depending on whether it is water- or spirit-based), but it is often cheaper to buy a ready-made primer.

spoiled for choice

The choice of paints available from decorating
stores is increasing rapidly and, as paints have
developed, the finishes available are now more
sophisticated than ever before. From suede-look to
glitter effects there are paints available to encourage
and inspire you to try something new on your walls.
It can cost little in time and money to create a new
look in your home.

paint
finishes

DON'T dismiss special paint effects as outdated. They can be the ideal solution for uneven or unlikely surfaces, adding color, texture, and interest, and creating the most sophisticated of looks without breaking the budget. There are plenty of paint finishes to suit the contemporary home, as well as the traditional one.

sponge

rag

steel wool

Here a picture provides the inspiration for sand colored colorwashed walls.

basics

The key to using paint finishes effectively is not to overdo them. Having mastered the techniques, don't succumb to the urge to display your skill on every surface in the house. Paint effects work most successfully when they are used to create a particular style, or either to disguise or emphasize a specific feature of a room. An ugly, uneven wall can be enhanced by a color wash, and a melamine bathroom unit can be transformed with a marble-look worktop, but adding extra stencils, stamps, or sponge work to the same room will lead to overkill.

Remember, also, only to treat a surface to a special effect if it could actually be made from the material you are faking. For example, marbling a wood-panelled door will only create a rather unlikely finish, whereas marbling a floor, wall, or fire place is much more reasonable. Even in the 19th century, those who couldn't afford it faked it—so why not follow in their footsteps? If you need inspiration, leaf through any books on grand traditional houses. Or, for a more relaxed look, take the lead from Mediterranean homes.

PREPARATION

Any surface you are going to cover with a special paint effect needs to be prepared. Some finishes, such as marbling, require a smoother surface

Two shades of blue on the walls provide a cohesiveness with the woodwork and the cloudy pattern of the tiles.

dragging brush

rocker

than, for example, colorwashing which can be used to cover rough plaster and will divert the eye from any irregularities in the wall.

Even if you are going to apply a colored oil glaze (see p. 38) you don't need to have an oil base coat on walls—vinyl silk latex is an ideal base. Woodwork, however, does need a base coat of an oil-based paint, such as eggshell.

At first, unless you are confident with color, start with a base coat of white or cream, then cover it with a colored glaze. Later you can try experimenting with colored base coats—either lighter or darker than the glaze you are going to apply.

MAINTENANCE

If a paint effect has been finished with acrylic varnish it will be quite durable and you will be able to wipe it down with a damp cloth and a mild cleanser to remove marks. However, if the surface is left unprotected you will need to be more careful. The advantage of colorwash paint effects is that the pattern is faded and irregular anyway so a small worn area will make little difference.

tools

Many paint effects can be achieved with basic tools—ordinary brushes, rollers, and even potatoes. But some finishes are easier with a special brush: for colorwashing try a soft brush, such as a badger, about 6in (15cm) wide; for dragging use a 6in (15cm) brush; and for wood graining, a brush with a long line of hairs (a horse-hair stippling brush).

Experiment with mixing two or more colors to achieve the shade you want.

MIXING A COLORED GLAZE

A glaze is used for most of the paint effects here. An easy colored glaze can be made using acrylic glaze (available from decorating centers), water and artist's oil colors. Mix the glaze and water in a paint kettle in a proportion of 3:1, then add the color, a little at a time. You will probably need to mix at least two different colors to get the shade you want. Stir well to work the color into the glaze. If the color is darker than you expected, add more glaze and water to make it lighter again.

Paint effects allow you to create the most fantastic and fanciful of effects—such as a burnished gold-colored hallway for those looking for a touch of grandeur.

VARNISH

To protect the paint finish you should cover it with two coats of varnish. Three types of varnish are available: flat, satin, and gloss. Any of these is suitable; it is up to you to decide how

shiny you want the finished surface to be. After applying the first coat, let it dry, then rub it down gently with wet-and-dry sandpaper soaked in water. If you take off any paint color, simply retouch it before applying the second coat of varnish.

A colorwashed wall is an informal finish that is ideal for family rooms.

READY-TO-PAINT FINISHES

If the idea of mixing oil colors and glazes is still daunting, don't worry. Manufacturers have recognized the need for a quicker and easier option. Just some of the options are thinned semi-transparent water-based paints that can be used from the can for sponging, colorwashing, and ragrolling; paints to create a woodwash effect, paints to create a metallic effect on walls, wood, or metal and even spray-on paints that create a stone effect.

glaze medium

crackle glaze

traditional paint effects

From the time that paint was first used to decorate a wall, people have experimented with different effects. All the paint effects on pages 40–43 are appropriate for a traditional home, or a room with a more traditional look. The key to success lies in choosing the right paint colors for your base coat, glaze, or stencil—steer clear of anything too bright. You want to give the impression that the paint has faded and softened with time. This does not mean you have to limit yourself to a palette of typical Victorian deep reds and greens. The Georgian palette, for example, was pale and serene. Look for subtle colors, though, with a matte finish.

dragging brush

artist's brush

COLORWASHING

This technique has a relaxed finish and looks effective no matter how pronounced or subtle your brushwork. You can use this effect in all but the most formal rooms. On a plastered wall, soft pinks and terracottas create an informal, rustic look, ideal for a "cottage" kitchen. On a smooth surface, colorwashing adds texture and a depth of color you cannot achieve with paint alone. Choose golden yellows for a welcoming living room or soft reds, pinks, or cinnamon for a warm, relaxing dining room. For full details see page 52.

The color you use dictates the feel of the room. Here fresh colors create a more modern look.

DRAGGING

This effect is perfect for period properties, producing a traditional look with a softer finish than simple paint can provide. However, it is not a suitable finish for uneven walls as the lines of the bristles will become distorted. It works particularly well as a finish below a chair rail and on doors, and it can be varnished for extra protection.

First paint the wall with vinyl silk latex—white is fine. Then apply a colored glaze (see p. 38) using a 6in (15cm) dragging brush, moving from the top of the wall to the base as smoothly as possible. Use a dry 6in (15cm) dragging brush to brush off some glaze, again working in a long, even movement from top to bottom. Brush on and brush off one strip at a time until you have covered a wall.

Dragging paintwork can create a wood-grained effect, adding interest to simple, cheap pieces of furniture.

Muted, pale colors work best for a more traditional look since they give the impression that the color has softened over time.

Paint effects can help to unite the surfaces in a room, transforming simple woodwork into something more grand.

marbling sponge

MARBLING

One of the oldest decorative painting techniques, marbling is referred to as a faux finish, since it creates the impression that a surface is made of a different material—in this case, marble. To achieve a convincing finish, you need to have studied the character and color of the real thing, or at least some good pictures of it. You don't have to be a slave to reality, though—a little bit of artistic license when it comes to the colors is fine, but keep the base coat, glaze, and veining fairly similar in terms of color and intensity to make the final effect more coherent. Paint a base coat of white oil-based paint. Mix a colored glaze (see p. 38) and paint it on to create the veins. Soften the edges with a sponge and brush with a dry brush to blend. Make the glaze a bit darker by adding more color and repeat the process. Finish off by going over the surface with a dry brush.

With a faux finish, remember the golden rule of only working on areas that might logically have been made from that material. If you are going to marble an entire wall, consider dividing the wall into slabs, then defining the edges with an artist's brush and a deeper tone glaze afterwards.

DISTRESSING

Sometimes new, pristine paint doesn't look quite right. When you want to create a home that looks as if it has been enjoyed by your family for centuries, your furniture and woodwork need to have the same aura. This is where distressing comes into its own, creating a finish that looks as if the wood has taken its fair share of knocks over the years.

steel wool

Distressing woodwork to reveal other colors below the surface creates a homey, rustic effect. It also gives the impression that the surface has been decorated and redecorated for generations.

First paint a base coat of eggshell, then cover it with a colored glaze (see p. 38). Before it dries, use steel wool to remove some of the glaze in the areas that would logically take more wear, then finish it with a coat of flat acrylic varnish. A similar look can be achieved using a base coat and top coat of different colored latex paints, then distressing the surface once it has dried with steel wool or even with an old set of keys for a more worn look.

contemporary paint effects

Modern paint effects are simple, but bold. There has been a move away from anything too fussy and floral, and in terms of palette, neutrals—from white to taupe—are increasingly featured.

PAINTED CHAIR RAIL

Painting the walls in two different colors above and below chair rail height immediately gives a room more interest. You don't need a traditional chair rail, you can just paint a stripe on the wall—either one simple line or give it more depth with a border stripe. Once the wall has been painted, mark the line or lines along it in pencil, using a ruler and plumb line to guide you. The chair rail line normally lies about 36in (90cm) above the baseboard, so position the top line at about this height around the room, with the lower line about 2in (5cm) below it. Stick low-tack masking tape along the outer edge of each line, then paint carefully between the lines. Peel

Careful preparation, having the correct tools and using guidelines, such as masking tape, to steady your line, will help you to achieve a more professional look.

You can give a room the effect of a traditional chair rail by using a simple, but effective, paint technique.

off the masking tape carefully while the paint is still damp and put on fresh tape before you apply a second coat.

PAINTING STRIPES

When painting stripes you can choose your own
color or even continue the stripes over wall units if
you are feeling bold. Precise finishes such as these
need careful preparation, however. First paint the
room with a base coat of latex in the lighter of the
two colors you have chosen. Decide what sort of
stripes you want—you could go for straight vertical
stripes or even wavy horizontal stripes.

Once you have decided you need to mark the
walls with pencil, giving yourself guidelines to paint
between. If you are painting vertical stripes, using a
plumb line will help you keep the marks straight,
and masking the outside of each strip with low-tack
tape will make painting easier. If you are painting
horizontal stripes, you simply mark pencil points
along the wall to help guide you.

*Hand-painted stripes provide
an informal look, offering you
a wider choice of color and
pattern than wallpaper.*

plumb line

Square shapes used as a decorative feature on the walls create a striking effect.

PAINTED PICTURE OF SQUARES

A light-colored, painted wall is the perfect base for some additional decoration, especially on a focal point such as a chimney piece or the wall above a sofa. Draw one large square, or perhaps four smaller ones, on your wall, measuring them accurately with a ruler, and mask the edges with low-tack tape. You might want to create a border around each square for extra definition, in which case you will need to draw another line around each square and mask that too.

Simple painted squares look dramatic, but if the rest of the room is plain, you could also consider decorating each square with a simple stamp or stencil (*see pp. 48 and 54*). Take care that the design is not too busy.

square stamps

EXPRESS YOURSELF

Why spend a fortune on expensive canvases when you can create your own works of art on the walls? You don't have to be a great artist to achieve a stunning effect. Choose a selection of matte latex paint colors that work well together, perhaps three or four colors from the same paint card sample. Draw out your "canvas" area on the wall and paint it in one of your chosen colors. Next paint a band of the second color near the top of the picture and soften the edges with a brush soaked in water. Add another one or two bands of different colors, again softening and blurring the edges with water. (Turn to the project on page 28 for a more daring interpretation of this technique.)

You can create your own masterpiece simply by painting bands of color onto the wall and blending in the edges. Modern art books are a good source of inspiration.

stencils and stamps

stencils

Sometimes a plain painted surface simply cries out for some extra decoration. Stencils and stamps are ideal in these situations, allowing you to add pattern or reinforce the theme of a room, while maintaining control over the colors, design, and amount of pattern you use in a way you simply cannot do with ready-patterned finishes, such as wallpaper.

Stenciling and stamping are two of the oldest decorating techniques—and the most simple too (see project on pp. 54–55). Make your own stencil designs by tracing or drawing patterns and cutting them out of stencil card or acetate or, if you are pushed for time or inspiration, you can buy ready-made stencils in art or decorating centers, along with special paint and stencil brushes to make the job easier. You can buy ready-made stamps, too, but why not revert to your school days and try making simple shapes from potatoes? Simply cut a potato in half, then carve a raised stamp by cutting away around the edges to make a shape. Far more satisfying!

The stenciled finishes favored in recent years have been quite restrained and rather precious—a trail of flowers running along a picture rail,

Stencils, which are enduringly popular, are a traditional way of decorating a wood floor.

perhaps, or numerous bunches of grapes repeated at chair rail height around the room. The 21st-century stencil or stamp is designed more simply and used more daringly— although in some ways with more restraint. Rather than covering every surface in a room with the same print, choose one area or wall and make a feature of it with simple shapes and bold colors. Instead of endlessly

repeating one small design, consider the effect of applying one large stenciled shape to an area. To make this easier and avoid having to cut out an unwieldy stencil, try using an overhead projector to project an enlarged version of your chosen image on to a wall, then trace the outline with a pencil before filling it in with color.

A child's room is the perfect place to make use of lots of stencils and stamps. Choose a theme for the room and then decorate walls and furniture.

To use a stencil to best effect, fix it to the wall with low-tack masking tape and hold the edge down as you paint to prevent paint from running

Stencils need not be floral and traditional—you can make them as abstract and contemporary as you like.

underneath it. Put very little latex paint on the brush to keep it dry, then apply the paint with a stippling rather than a flowing action. If you vary the intensity of the color within the out-line of the stencil the finish is more textured than if you fill it with a uni-form amount of paint. Once the stencil has been removed, you can add color by hand for extra detail.

combining

paint effects

This chapter has already shown how versatile special paint effects can be and hopefully dispelled any lingering misconceptions that they are the sort of finish you only see in flowery cottage-style interiors. Paint finishes can be used to enhance any home, from the 19th-century Victorian to the 21st-century loft conversion, working with every sort of material, from bare stone to cork tiling.

However, try to avoid overkill and use paint finishes in moderation. Pick out one surface and decorate that, then keep everything else in that room relatively simple. A room will look good with colorwashed walls, but avoid adding lots of other effects around the room.

For a Mediterranean look combine colorwashed walls with terracotta flooring, white or natural woodwork, and simple wooden furniture.

A more contemporary effect can be achieved by keeping most of the walls white or fresh, then making a feature out of one wall. You could try painting a modern art design on it, or perhaps try the blended stripe effect shown on pp. 28–29. For either of these to look effective you will need to combine them with other modern finishes, pale wood flooring, glass-topped tables, and sleek furniture.

If you are talented with a paintbrush, why not copy the theme or patterns of the wallpaper onto the woodwork to create a unified look?

Here the wooden drawers and elegant chair combine with classical ornaments to suggest that a look has evolved rather than been designed.

Distressing furniture helps you create the "shabby chic" effect that is an enduring favorite (see pp. 30–31). It allows you to mix pieces from all eras, so that the room really looks as if it has evolved over the years. It works especially well in neutral shades of white, cream, and muted pastels. Combine the painted furniture with traditional wooden pieces, comfortable sofas, wooden floorboards, and homey rugs. The walls will work with subtle faded wallpaper designs, plain painted walls in neutral or muted shades, or even a colorwash.

If the natural shades of wood don't suit the style of your home, they can still be transformed with paint to create more modern, cool colored, or homey effects.

A COLORWASHED WALL

Soft color applied with wide, relaxed strokes creates a surface treatment that works equally well on uneven walls or smooth plaster. Estimate the quantity of paint you will need by measuring the area you want to colorwash, allowing 1 pint (half a liter) to cover 6yd². Choose your pigment from a specialty shop, and experiment with color concentration before you mix the final glaze. Colorwashing is easiest if you can enlist the help of a friend.

INGREDIENTS

- *Vinyl silk latex*
- *Oil glaze (see p. 38)*
- *Ultramarine violet pigment for coloring*
- *Large plastic container with lid*
- *2 broad (6in/15cm) paintbrushes*
- *Clean rags*

METHOD

■ Give the surface of the wall a coat of vinyl silk latex in your chosen base color (here we used vinyl white silk). Leave to dry.

■ Mix up some tiny quantities of glaze and try them out in a corner of the room, near the baseboard. Keep a note of the quantities of pigment you use, so you have a recipe when you are happy with the color (to achieve the color on the wall opposite, we used 10oz [280g] of pigment to 6 pints [3 liters] of oil glaze.) When you have a sample you are pleased with, mix the complete quantity of glaze.

■ Working quickly, in broad strokes, start applying the glaze in the top right-hand corner of the wall, working outwards and downwards. Start going from right to left, then work over the area going from left to right, until you have covered a patch about a yard (a meter) square. Avoid making too regular a shape—if the edges dry before you paint the next patch, it's better if you don't leave an obvious line.

square stamps

metallic paint

STAMPING A WALL

Dull hallways, dining rooms, bathrooms, and, of course, children's rooms, are ideal places for adding detail. The shapes you use dictate the mood, creating a look that is anything from quirky to sophisticated. Stamped designs tend to be bolder and simpler than their stenciled counterparts: These silver squares stand out strongly against a rich blue wall.

INGREDIENTS

- Indigo vinyl eggshell paint
- Medium brush
- White pencil
- Plumb line
- Square stamp measuring 3in² (7.5cm²)
- Square stamp measuring 1in² (2.5cm²)
- Small can of metallic silver craft paint
- Shallow plastic dish or saucer

METHOD

■ Paint the wall with your chosen base color. A deep shade such as dark blue, red, or orange would work well in a dining room or a hallway and gives a dramatic contrast with the metallic silver squares.

■ When the paint is dry, measure your wall and decide how far apart you want your stamps to be spaced. Use the plumb line to measure straight lines down the wall as a guide for your stamps, making faint pencil marks top, bottom, and midway. (Here, the big stamps are placed at intervals of 4in [10 cm] apart, the

smaller squares are stamped between them, measured by eye to avoid too even an effect.)

■ Pour a small quantity of the silver paint into the plastic dish. Dip the larger stamp in it and experiment on some newspaper until you can get an even, square effect. Starting from the top left-hand corner of the wall, and, working from top to bottom, place the first row of the larger squares.

■ Continue stamping rows of the larger squares until the wall is covered. Then, working carefully by eye, place rows of smaller squares between them. It is best to wait until the large squares are dry before starting to stamp the smaller ones, to avoid smudging your work as you go.

FINISH	APPLICATIONS
STENCILING Creating a repeated pattern by painting over a cut-out design	The pattern you choose for your stencil should suit the style of the room. For a traditional room choose classical or floral motifs, and for modern rooms opt for something more simple, such as a geometric shape. In traditional rooms stenciling looks most effective if it is faded slightly, as if it has been there for some time. Choose muted colors and dab the paint on lightly with a stencil brush rather than filling in the stencil with solid blocks of color. Latex paint works well, though special-purpose stencil paints are now available in small cans.
STAMPING Using a raised stamp, such as a potato or readymade stamp, to decorate a wall	This is a good finish for plain walls painted with latex, creating a patterned, but personalized "wallpaper" effect. Stamping can also draw attention to a feature, such as a window, by stamping an outline around it, or a "chair rail" can be created by stamping a pattern at chair height around a room. Whereas stencils offer the opportunity to use several colors within one pattern, each stamped mark you make can only consist of one color, although you could alternate the colors you use on the stamp if you wish.
COLORWASHING A wash of latex paint color diluted with water, loosely brushed onto a wall with random strokes	This is a good paint effect for adding color to walls in a subtle and varied manner. It is suitable for walls that are rather uneven as the variation in the depth of color helps to conceal the irregularities below. It also helps to create an aged Mediterranean look, especially if you use colors used in sunny climates, such as terracotta and soft pink. Experiment with the thickness of your wash until you find the depth of color that you want.

FINISH	APPLICATIONS
MARBLING A paint effect simulating the color and markings characteristic of marble	For best results, only use this effect on areas that might genuinely be made of marble, such as fire places, paneling, bathroom fixtures, and floors. That said, it is unlikely that an amateur painter will achieve a look that may actually deceive people, so it is best to tackle it from a slightly "tongue in cheek" approach. If you want to make it as lifelike as possible, try copying a real piece of marble so that you can study the color and grain and emulate it with artists' oil colors.
DISTRESSING Creating an aged paint effect on woodwork and furniture	Solid pieces of furniture such as tables, closets, cupboards, and doors are ideal for this effect. It gives the impression that the pieces have been around for years and had several different coats of paint which, over the course of time, have become knocked and worn to reveal the older colors below. You can use layers of different colored latex or oil-based paint, then "age" the surface, by rubbing it with steel wool. Finally, protect it with varnish.
DRAGGING Fine lines achieved by removing wet paint or glaze with a brush or comb to reveal color beneath	Perfect for period properties, producing a traditional look with a softer finish than simple paint can provide. Dragging is not recommended for uneven walls as the lines of the bristles will become distorted. It works particularly well below a chair rail and on doors, and it can be varnished for extra protection.
SPONGING A broken color paint effect created by dabbing on paint or glaze with a natural marine sponge	An easy paint effect for walls in less formal rooms, such as a bedroom, bathroom, or child's room. The sponge produces a pattern that is useful for camouflaging irregular surfaces. Paint the wall with a base coat, then apply a second coat of a different paint color or glaze with the sponge, keeping it quite thin (four parts latex to one part water).

fashion

As fashions change, so do paint finishes. Just as colorwashing and stamping have recently become more popular than sponging and stenciling, the next new trend is sure to be just around the corner. The good news is that paint manufacturers are very aware of this and are continually developing products that will enable you to achieve the hottest new look for your home quickly, cheaply, and easily.

plaster & concrete

FOR YEARS we have covered, colored, and variously dressed our walls and floors, but today there is increased awareness of the natural beauty of plaster and concrete. From the loft apartment to the 18th-century mansion, any home can benefit from the bare honesty of these materials.

basics

PLASTER

Plastering is a complex technique that is usually only tackled by an expert. If you have never attempted it before, it is advisable to seek professional advice and to work closely with the plasterer to achieve precisely the effect you want. There are two main types of plaster: gypsum plaster and mixes based on cement, lime, and sand. They are classified as either base-coat plasters or topcoat plasters.

gypsum

lime

■ **GYPSUM PLASTER** This, the most common type of plaster, is produced from ground gypsum rock, which sets hard when mixed with water to create a good surface for interior walls. Base-coat gypsum plasters are pre-mixed with lightweight aggregates and only need water to be ready for use.

plaster

■ **LIME/CEMENT PLASTER** Before the advent of gypsum plasters, lime and sand plasters were used for undercoats, and neat lime for finishing. Base-coat sanded plasters based on lime and cement have to be mixed on site with sharp sand.

bonding agent

■ **ONE-COAT PLASTER** This is perhaps the easiest type of plaster to use in the home since it can be bought ready-mixed or in mixing tubs. For large areas buy large bags of plaster and mix it with water on site. For repairs, ready-mixed plasters are ideal. Before applying plaster you must prepare the surface you are treating

sand

with a bonding agent, which will improve the sticking power of the plaster. A low-absorption surface such as brick should be coated with a mix of one part bonding agent to five parts water, followed by a coat of four parts bonding agent to one part water. The plaster should be applied while the bonding is still tacky.

Utility meets decoration. A concrete floor can be decorated with floor paint to create the pattern of your choice. Here it has been given a naive tiled look with small blocks of color.

CONCRETE

A blend of cement, aggregate, and sand, concrete can be mixed and laid directly in the home or bought in slabs, blocks, and tiles. Traditionally it was used as a sub-floor or in utility areas, but these days concrete is screeded, waxed, textured, and painted to transform it into a flooring and wall choice that is very "now."

MAINTENANCE

Unfinished plaster will absorb anything that it comes into contact with so it can be hard to keep clean, but once sealed and polished or varnished, it can easily be cleaned with a little mild cleanser and a damp cloth. For instructions on how to seal and protect plaster or concrete see p. 66.

textured plaster

wire brush

spatula

Texture is big news in the home. So, you've already gathered a good mix of chenille, satin, and cotton to finish your sofa and chairs, but what about your walls? Ready-mixed wall coatings are currently riding on the crest of a wave with the renewed interest in textured surfaces. Once reviled, they are now available in a number of varieties and colors and can be finished in an almost infinite number of patterns to create the look you want.

If you can't quite bring yourself to slap on the ready-mix, think what you might do with traditional plaster. To encourage your imagination, let your mind wander the globe and draw inspiration from the stuccoes of Italy, the uneven wall finishes of rural

Rough plastered walls suit a modern interior as well as a more traditional, rustic one.

Spain and Morocco, or even the weather-beaten facades of New England. For a rustic, ethnic, or southern Mediterranean effect, choose a relaxed uneven pattern. To achieve a look that's more contemporary, opt for a more regular pattern and throw in some added texture in the form of shiny metals or stones (see p. 64).

In this living room, the rough texture of the plaster provides a successful contrast to the smooth lines of the wood and the softness of the sofa.

There are no rules when it comes to creating texture in plaster. Since the era of cave-dwelling, people have found their own unique ways of expressing themselves on their wall surfaces and creating a form of decoration that appeals to them. Be guided by the style of your home and your own personal taste rather than fashion.

If you are using plaster, either call in a professional to do the initial work and then add your own detail before the plaster has dried, or add a coat of finishing plaster to the walls yourself (after bonding them, see pp. 60–61) and let your creativity come to the fore. If you buy a textured coating, it is quite easy to do it yourself. Create spots, swirls, and lines, stipple it with a damp sponge, or experiment with a wire brush.

sponge

TIP

Textured plaster holds more dust than does a smooth surface, so be prepared to work hard to keep it clean.

creating your own effects

For the truly creative person, buying something off the shelf is never good enough because it is not unique. If simple plaster and cement do not offer the designer touch you hanker for, add it yourself. It is easy to do so, both at the mixing stage and once the plaster has been applied, but is still wet. Don't feel that you have to treat the whole room in the same way. Use special finishes to make a feature of one wall, half a wall, or just an alcove.

Plastered or concrete walls and floors lend themselves to added decoration when the newly laid surface is still wet. Shells, pebbles, and colored marbles are all perfect little treasures to set into the surface to achieve a unique, eye-catching finish.

IMAGINATIVE MIXES

Add colored pigments to the finishing plaster to create an attractive finish. This is a good way of creating a traditional plaster color of soft pinks and terracottas, with brand new plaster. For a more contemporary look, you can buy plaster ready-mixed in color finishes.

Add extra sand to the finishing plaster for a more grainy, textured look. Start cautiously, until you have a consistency you are happy with. Similarly, small particles of glass or shiny metals added to the plaster mix will help to give walls a reflective shimmering quality, especially in artificial light. Japanese-style interiors are often given extra

interest by mixing crushed shells, hemp fibers, or tiny white pebbles with the plaster.

For a floor that is not unlike terrazzo in finish, you can add a special aggregate to the cement mix. Then, after it has set, polish the floor to achieve a smooth, marble-like effect. This is best done by a professional to ensure a successful finish.

Once plaster or concrete has been applied to the surface, you can add interest and texture with anything that can withstand the wear. A line of pebbles embedded into the floor around the edge of a room works well, or try making a pattern across the surface with blocks of beach pebbles. On a wall, inset a group of four ceramic tiles for a dramatic statement, or score a pattern with a blunt tool— perhaps creating the impression of stone blocks.

A coat of whitewash is a traditional finish for rough plastered walls and is perfect for achieving a traditional or Mediterranean look.

sealing and protecting

resin varnish

New plaster can take up to six weeks to dry thoroughly, during which time efflorescence, which is caused by alkaline deposits, will leak out onto the surface. Use a stiff brush to remove these deposits every now and then until they stop appearing. Only then should you seal and/or protect the walls.

If you want to give added depth to the plaster with a colorwash or any special paint finish, it needs to be sealed first to give the paint something to adhere to. Whether you decide to paint the wall or leave the plaster in its natural state, the surface needs to be protected to prevent dust coming off on your hands when you touch it.

varnish brush

SEALING PLASTER AND CONCRETE

If you want to cover new plaster with an oil paint, you need to prime it with an alkali-resistant primer. If you use a latex paint to finish it, seal it with a fine coat of latex thinned with water, applied with a brush or roller.

Concrete doesn't need priming if you are going to paint it with a special-purpose floor paint. Painted a glossy color, in a neutral tone, such as white, off-white, or black, concrete can make a really

The natural pink hue of new plaster is soft, warm, and attractive, but it needs to be sealed if the surface is to be protected from stains.

sophisticated floor with a sheen to help reflect the light—ideal for kitchens, but also good for a chic or utilitarian-style living room.

PROTECTING THE SURFACE

For walls, the best varnish is non-yellowing and water based. Choose flat, satin, or gloss to suit the style of your home. On natural-looking, pinky plaster, a flat varnish will probably work best, whereas a glossy varnish will look good if you want a shiny modern look with a reflective quality. Give a concrete floor several coats of acrylic varnish to make it tough and resistant. This is important in high-traffic areas or in places such as kitchens, where you may use strong detergents to keep the floor clean.

In line with fashion, a textured ceiling is something many of us now try to avoid, but when combined with wood in a rustic setting the effect looks completely appropriate.

polishing and waxing

drill

polishing mop

polishing disc

Bare plaster can achieve a really lovely sheen once it has been polished or waxed. Polishing is good in areas where you just want to make the most of the inherent colors of the plaster, whereas waxing also gives the surface protection against wear and tear.

POLISHING AND COLORING

There is no real art to polishing a plaster wall, just physical effort. Hard rubbing with a soft cloth is the simplest—but not necessarily the easiest—way. If the wall is large, you may wish to use an electric hand tool with a special polishing attachment. (If this all sounds like too much effort—and it is hard work—you can achieve a similar effect with a coat of acrylic varnish.)

This bathroom wall has been roughly plastered and given a colorwash finish. A simple line drawing on a grand scale was added before it was finally polished or varnished.

A polished plaster finish is most suited to interiors based on traditional Italian style. For an even more authentic look, mix oil colors in shades of yellow ocher, burnt umber, raw umber, and gray into the plaster before you apply it. When it is dry, sand and then polish it with a soft lint-free cloth until it gains a gentle, but dull sheen. For a grand Italian villa style, keep the colors paler and more subtle—natural plaster perhaps with an extra tint of pink—and again polish it to a soft shine.

soft polishing brushes

lint free cloth

Make the most of any artistic talent you have by painting your own fresco.

WAXING PLASTER

Choose a suitable ready-made wax—one containing a blend of beeswax and carnuba is ideal. Unless you want to make the surface more yellow or brown, the wax should be as translucent as possible to allow the existing colors to shine through, so avoid tinted waxes. Some waxes contain silicones to make them tougher and easier to polish to a high gloss (although that may not be the look you want).

Bare plaster is best sealed first with a bonding agent to stop the wax being absorbed too deeply. Once it is dry you can start waxing. Work with a cloth pad and rub in a circular motion. After applying a couple of coats, leave it for several hours to harden, then buff it with a soft shoe-cleaning brush. Finish polishing with a soft duster. This is hard work, so you may want to employ a professional.

plaster

combining

Plaster can work in any style of room—provided you get the color and/or texture right. Here is a rundown of a few basic types of plaster and the styles to which they are best suited.

Rough, unevenly textured plaster (such as that seen in the project on pages 74–75) is best suited to Moroccan or rural-style rooms, where the feeling is relaxed. For a Moroccan finish, combine the rough plaster look with earthy paint shades, or white-washed walls, and decorate the room with kilims on the floor, naive metal work, multicolored glass, and elaborately carved woodwork.

Bare, simple walls help to create a sense of calm minimalism in a room where the only comfort is provided by cushions.

To achieve a rural "cottage" look, combine the rough plaster finish with soft earthy colors or whitewash, exposed brickwork, aged dark wood, bare stone, and earthenware.

Textured plaster with a dimpled surface suits interiors that are more contemporary, in which the emphasis is on simplicity and texture. Combine this sort of plaster finish with bleached wood floors, white paint, large expanses of glass, and functional furniture.

The rough textured walls work well in this earthy, rustic-style kitchen featuring wooden fixtures and a tiled floor.

Smooth waxed plaster walls are more evocative of a shabby chic, largely European, style. They exude an aura of faded grandeur, so combine them with cool traditional ceramic floor tiles, expensive wood furniture, and marble. To finish the look, go for classic fabrics with a hint of luxury, such as old velvet, silk, damask, or toile de Jouy.

A polished concrete floor looks good in contemporary, slightly utilitarian surroundings. In a kitchen it works well with plenty of stainless steel appliances and surfaces, glass blocks, and white or bright paint colors on the walls. In a living room or dining space, it is flexible but suits a more minimalist look. This is not a floor treatment to combine with flowers and frills. Metal, glass, simple tiles, and bleached wood all make good partners for a polished concrete floor.

The soft blue-gray tones of the plastered walls blend in well with the wooden kitchen worktops. The flowers add a splash of color.

TINTING AND POLISHING PLASTER

Unless you are experienced in DIY, plaster finishes are best undertaken with the help of an expert. Either work with your decorator on this and the following project (you can create the tint and do the polishing; the decorator can be in charge of applying the plaster evenly) or ask if he or she will teach you how to skim a plaster wall successfully. Adding extra color to plaster before it is applied allows you to create a wide variety of effects.

INGREDIENTS

- *One-coat plaster (your plasterer will advise on how much you will need)*
- *1lb 1oz (500g) red oxide pigment*
- *Bonding adhesive*
- *Large can of beeswax*
- *Clean, soft cloths for buffing*

METHOD

■ Mix a cupful of plaster and experiment with tinting, dropping in tiny quantities of pigment. The color will fade by about 50 percent as the plaster dries, so create a mix that is darker than the color you want. When you are happy with your shade, get your plasterer to mix up the whole quantity and tint it to match. (1lb 1oz of pigment was enough to color the plaster richly for 44yds^2 [40m^2] for the room opposite.)

■ If you have the expertise, apply the plaster in a thin, even layer or ask your plasterer to do it. Leave it until it is dry.

■ Mix a thin coat of bonding adhesive (6 parts water to 1 part bonding agent) to seal the wall and stop it absorbing too much wax. Paint this quickly and evenly over the wall. Leave to dry.

■ Take a small amount of beeswax on a clean cloth and, starting from the top left-hand corner, rub it into the plaster thoroughly, working on an area about a yard (meter) square at a time. When the first layer has been worked in, apply a second coat. Work slowly and thoroughly —too much wax applied too quickly will lead to a blotchy effect.

■ When the second coat is complete, buff the wall with a soft rag until it attains a soft sheen. This is hard work, but the resulting finish is a rich, luxuriant gleam.

■ If you want to take a shortcut, apply a thin coat of gloss acrylic varnish instead of the beeswax. The result will be attractive, although it will lack the depth of finish of beeswax.

PATTERNING PLASTER

Give a room a truly individual finish by marking patterns in the plaster yourself, either by hand or with a simple tool. Unless you are experienced at DIY, you will need a professional to apply the plaster. Explain the effect you want to achieve, then move in as soon as the plaster is complete, but while it is still damp. The pattern shown here will suit a variety of styles, from the rustic to the contemporary minimalist. Lines or spirals are the simplest effects to achieve.

INGREDIENTS

■ One-coat plaster
■ String
■ Push pins
■ Spatula or pencil, for marking patterns
■ Matte varnish
■ Medium paintbrush

METHOD

■ Decide where you want your lines, how they should be grouped, and how many there should be. Make pencil marks at the outer corners of the wall to mark the starting points of each line, measuring so that they are at an even height at each end. Cut some lengths of string wider than the wall, and have these and some push pins ready to use as soon as the wall is plastered.

■ Either apply a coat of finishing plaster to the wall, or get your professional helper to do it. It should be left slightly rough, but should be even and flat.

■ As soon as the plastering is complete, fix lengths of string across the wall, using push pins to fix them in the corners, matching the pencil marks to ensure they are straight. Then run a spatula or pencil lightly along them, keeping the line as straight as possible. (Alternatively mark spirals with a finger quickly all over the surface—see below.)

■ Leave the plaster to dry. It can be finished with a thin coat of matte varnish, brushed on with a medium-sized paintbrush.

FINISH	APPLICATIONS
UNFINISHED PLASTER Bare plaster, left unsealed	A basic finish only appropriate for rooms that get minimal wear and tear as the unsealed plaster surface easily absorbs any marks and it is impossible to remove them. A good choice for an adult's bedroom, creating a romantic, traditional pink effect.
TINTED PLASTER Raw plaster with added color	See above for notes about the practicality of this surface. The only difference here is that this plaster has a pigment added to the mix to give it a hint of color.
POLISHED PLASTER Plaster polished to a soft or high sheen	Once treated with a beeswax mixture or a soft silicon polish, the odd mark can be polished away, but this is still a rather high maintenance finish that is best suited to rooms that get only light use. It takes a lot of work and several layers of polish to achieve a good effect.
VARNISHED PLASTER Plaster sealed with matte or gloss varnish	This is a more practical, low maintenance version of polished plaster, but the effect is more even and slightly less 'natural' looking. Gloss varnished plaster works best in rooms that get a lot of use, such as kitchens, as it is easier to wipe clean.
LIMEWASH An old-fashioned wash for plaster, made from a mix of lime, water, and coloring	An old-fashioned type of white paint that is tricky to use as it requires constant stirring. It creates a rough, rustic effect and has a tendency to flake, but the soft, powdery matte texture is very attractive. Some pigments will react to the lime so refer to the manufacturers' instructions before adding color.

FINISH	APPLICATIONS
DISTEMPER Often referred to as whitewash. Like limewash but with an even softer, flakier finish	A fragile but beautiful finish. It comes off easily to the touch, and so wears very badly. Use it only in rooms that get occasional use.
FRESCO Plaster painted with watercolor while still wet	Good for a simple, naive interior. You can create patterns on the plaster, such as rough stripes, squares, or spots, with the watercolor, . The paint must be applied while the plaster is still wet. The finish must be varnished when it is dry or it has a tendency to flake away.
TEXTURED PLASTER Plaster worked on with texturing tools while it is still wet	Good for both modern or very traditional cottage-style rooms, this technique allows you to create patterns with texture in the wall surface itself. When the plaster is applied to the wall make your mark on it with combs, rollers, or even your fingers. The surface is difficult to varnish afterward, so it is best used in areas where it can be kept bare or simply painted.

popular plaster

Throughout history plaster has been an essential surface material, and its qualities will undoubtedly continue to be appreciated throughout the 21st century. From simple whitewash to bare pink and more vividly colored plasters, this surface has a charm that is well suited to both traditional and modern interiors.

wallcoverings

WALLCOVERINGS have nudged their way back into fashion—and deservedly so. If the rest of your furnishings are plain, wallcoverings are a good way of injecting pattern as well as color into your room, and the motif you choose will help to reinforce your style or theme.

basics

Wallcoverings can transform an interior completely—their color, pattern, and even texture all influence the mood, style, or theme of the room. When choosing a wallcovering, however, consider not only its aesthetic qualities but also its practical aspects, such as durability and washability.

With paste, a brush, and some paper, you can add both color and pattern to a room, almost instantly.

UNDERSTANDING WALLCOVERINGS

It is now possible to buy a wallcovering to suit almost any purpose and style.

■ **LINING PAPER** This is a base for wallpaper or paint, which provides a better surface if walls are uneven or if the final wallpaper is to be of very high quality. It is hung horizontally.

You can be nearly as creative with wallpaper as you can with paint. Here a second colorway from the same wallpaper collection has been hung horizontally to create a more dramatic, modern take on the wallpaper border.

■ **PRINTED WALLPAPER** Machine-printed paper is the most common type of wallpaper, offering the widest range of patterns and colors. It can often be

sponged, but is not recommended for heavy-duty areas such as children's rooms and kitchens.

■ **PAPER-BACKED VINYL** A film of plastic makes this wallpaper stronger and more washable. It is useful for areas, such as bathrooms, where condensation is a problem.

■ **SPONGEABLE** Although not as durable as vinyl papers, these are coated with a thin plastic film so they can be wiped with a damp cloth.

■ **WALLPAPER BORDERS** There are two types: self-adhesive and those needing paste. A border is a quick and easy way of adding pattern and creating a theme. It draws attention to the proportions of the room, though, so has the effect of lowering a ceiling.

■ **PRE-PASTED PAPER** This has a backing of dried paste, which is activated by soaking it in water.

■ **TEXTURED AND EMBOSSED** The relief patterns on this heavyweight paper add interest while hiding uneven walls below. Types include Anaglypta —embossed paper—and Vinaglypta —an embossed vinyl. You can finish these papers with paint.

■ **PAPER-BACKED FABRICS** Fabrics can be given a paper backing. You may need special adhesive and you must be careful not to get paste on the surface of the fabric.

■ **WOODCHIP TEXTURED** With small pieces of wood, this covering helps conceal imperfections in the wall below. It needs to be painted.

Despite the patterned paper, the look here is not too "busy" since the accent color of the wallpaper matches the drapes.

MAINTENANCE

Every wallpaper you buy now should come with intructions on the label to indicate how it should be cared for, so keep a note of these. It's a good idea to test a small area first before using a cleaning product on the paper, but most marks can be removed with a clean artists' rubber or even a piece of bread rubbed over any dirty marks. Washable wallpapers and vinyls can be wiped with a damp sponge.

textured papers

textured samples

Textured wall coverings are an easy and effective way of adding a dash of both texture and pattern to any room. Relief patterned wallpapers no longer need to be confined to the traditional home—the new collections have been designed with the contemporary interior very much in mind. There are over 150 designs of embossed wallpaper alone, including plaster effects, natural weaves, and period stripes, as well as more eye-catching designs such as old English script, crackle glaze, and funky swirls.

This space is given the added dimension of textural interest, which complements the simplicity of the neutral color scheme and simple furniture.

The practical, forgiving nature of these papers, and the fact that they can be repainted time after time, makes them an ideal choice for hallways, playrooms, and other areas that are subject to a lot of

wear and tear. You don't have to decorate the entire room with the same paper—you could paper only one wall or just the area below the chair rail.

HOW TO USE THEM

The great thing about this type of wallcovering is that it is intended to be finished with your own choice of paint, so you can create a surface that is as subtle or dramatic as you wish. Before you start thinking about finishes, though, you need to prepare the walls by hanging lining paper horizontally on them. Next, cover the back of the textured paper with plenty of heavy-duty paste, allowing it to soak in. Once you have positioned the paper correctly on the wall and smoothed out any bubbles, use a damp cloth to gently smooth down the seams—a roller will flatten the pattern.

The textured paper in this hallway can be repainted periodically to give the area a fresh look at minimal cost.

colored wallcoverings

colored samples

If you like the look of plain painted walls, but the surface is too uneven or you need something more washable, don't despair. Plenty of wallpaper collections now offer what is essentially a paint effect on a roll. Perfect for anyone who wants to avoid brushes, tints, and glazes, these papers re-create anything from a simply painted wall to a sponged, dragged, or multi-colorwashed interior. The colors available are, of course, dictated by fashion trends, so you have less flexibility than if you mix paint colors yourself, but, that said, the selection is not at all limited. Currently you can find colors ranging from soft organic colors, based on natural dyes, to the deep intense hues of fall and the fresh spring shades of lime green, citrus yellow, and pale lilac. Translucency is also a key look for surfaces now, so many wallcoverings are being given a gentle gleaming glaze to reflect as much light as possible into your room.

The subtle patterning of this paper adds further interest to the room, softening the overall effect more than a plain painted wall would.

HOW TO USE THEM

These sorts of wallpaper are great for decorating an entire room, as well as for mixing and matching with patterned papers and paint. Rather than committing yourself to a room that is entirely plain or

entirely patterned, create added interest and make a feature of certain areas by giving them a different treatment than the other surfaces. For instance, if you have fallen in love with a boldly patterned wallcovering, but think it might be too much on every wall of the room, why not use it to finish one focal wall, such as behind the sideboard, the sofa, or the bed, then choose a coordinating colored wallpaper for the other walls?

When it comes to choosing a color, go back to the rules of color theory and the color wheel on page 24 for inspiration and suggestions on what sort of color would suit your particular room. If you've already settled on your curtain or blind fabric, select a wallcovering that will highlight rather than contrast with the main fabric color to make the overall look more harmonious.

A contemporary design and a warm red wallcovering complement the modern furniture in this room.

small-patterned samples

patterned wallcoverings

Trends for wallpaper patterns come and go, but whatever the motif, the designs can be divided into two categories: large- and small-patterned.

SMALL-PATTERNED WALLCOVERINGS

Linking the scale of the pattern to the size of the area you are decorating is important, but you do not have to limit yourself to small motifs simply because the room you are decorating is not large. A room decorated in a small-scale pattern will appear more spacious, but a tiny guest lavatory can look striking with one wall papered in a large pattern.

Mixing the scale of the patterns within a room helps to maintain a sense of balance, while continuing the floral motif creates a unity of theme and look.

HOW TO USE THEM

It is hard to imagine a pattern *in situ*, especially when wallpapers are viewed in sample books that are a fraction of the size of the wall they will cover. Even patterns that appear large in the sample look smaller on the wall. One trick is to prop the book against the wall and view it from the farthest position in the room. Some small repeat motifs lose their identity and blur into a general pattern. This is ideal if you want the wallcovering to serve as a subtle foil to a set of pictures, say, rather than making a statement of its own, but if you want your motif to have more impact, you will need to choose something on a larger scale.

Spotted wallcoverings are fun and lively, but a plain wallcovering on the lower half of the wall prevents the overall effect from being too busy.

small-patterned samples

LARGE-PATTERNED PAPERS

If small-scale patterns create a subtle backdrop for bolder elements, then large-scale patterns obviously make more of a statement and reduce the apparent size of a room, so they need to be handled a little more cautiously. That said, a bold pattern used with style can look fantastic.

HOW TO USE THEM

Some wallcoverings can have a reasonably large motif, but because the color of the motif is quite cool or subtle or blends well with the background, it has less of an impact and can be used without fear of overpowering the room. Or try a design in which you can "see through" the motif, such as a trellis or an open, flowing line. Wallcoverings decorated with a mixture of small and large shapes are often less

large-patterned samples

The large-scale stripe of this wallpaper echoes the pattern on the sofa and complements the large motifs on the fabric hangings. A small-patterned wallpaper would be overshadowed and feel too busy for the simple drama of this room.

It can be hard to mix and match some patterns. Here the same pattern is repeated on the drapes and the bed linen.

A large-scale floral pattern with an open background is gentle on the eye and ideal for a bedroom.

obtrusive than those with a repeated large motif.

Stripes are generally classified as a big pattern, yet very narrow stripes will appear as a blur in a softer color than the stripe itself when seen from a distance, and will therefore lose their impact. Conversely, broad stripes, particularly in two colors, will draw in the room, making it appear smaller than it is. Vertical stripes undoubtedly add height to the walls, but for a more contemporary look, consider hanging the paper horizontally and increase the apparent width of the room.

Geometric patterns, such as stripes, circles, and squares, are enjoying a revival and look great in any room. There is also a trend for large flower and leaf shapes, which can look good in a living room or dining room, not just a bedroom, if used with flair. The secret of success lies in toning down "excesses" in some areas and using more subtlety in others. Save your bold designs for one key wall or alcoves, for example, and use a coordinating plain color on the other walls. But make sure that an alcove is big enough to feature enough of the pattern, and ensure that the pattern is central on a large wall by starting at the focal point, such as the chimney piece.

themed wallcoverings

trompe-l'oeil samples

Since prehistoric times people have used pictorial representations to decorate their homes, depicting images and scenes from everyday life, history, and, more recently, children's films and books. From medieval tapestries and 18th-century toile de Jouy, with its scenes of rural life, to Barbie and Winnie the Pooh, pictorial wallcoverings will place your room firmly in a particular era or film set. Be warned—pictorial patterns will give a room a very definite theme, but they can also dominate.

HOW TO USE THEM

As with any large-patterned paper, you need to be aware of the scale of the room and the impact of the pattern in it. In some rooms you can afford to be daring with a pictorial pattern. Bathrooms and children's bedrooms or playrooms, for example, are ideal places to introduce large-scale scenes, but rooms you spend a lot of time in should be treated more cautiously. When you are surrounded by Greek urns day and night they lose their appeal.

Try introducing the themed wallcovering in selected areas— one wall or a couple of alcoves, perhaps. Or consider how you

A classic motif works best in a traditional interior that has not only the space to accommodate it, but also the furniture to complement it.

could create an area in which to display the wall-covering without allowing it to dominate. Create a "picture frame" either with wooden moldings or a wallpaper border and cut a piece of wallcovering to fit inside. Or cut out elements of the wallpaper and use them decoupage-style to decorate a closet door, topped with layers of non-yellowing varnish.

If you haven't got it, fake it. Here a false fireplace has been created with some clever trompe l'oeil paper.

The script theme of this bathroom has been continued with the accessories—two giant letters of the alphabet.

However you use a themed wallcovering, you cannot do it half-heartedly. If the theme isn't continued elsewhere in the room, the treated surface will just look out of place. Repeat the theme in some small way on your soft fur-nishings or in your accessories, but don't overdo it either—you are treading a rather fine line.

Here the chair rail and the wall beneath are painted in different colors, both of which appear in the wallpaper pattern.

combining

Like paint, wallcoverings are an extremely versatile finish and will work well with almost any other material—as long as the covering you choose is in a color and style to complement its surroundings. Before choosing a wallcovering for your room, think about the mood or style that its color and pattern suggest. If the pattern is regular and formal, it will not sit easily with rustic, unsophisticated materials, such as rough stone, unglazed tiles, and bare plaster, unless you are a confident and creative designer. Instead, think of combining it with paintwork in a similar tone—perhaps picking out a color in the pattern—and other classic materials such as ceramic tiles and polished wood.

Certain patterns are evocative of a particular style, country, or era, and by choosing one you are essentially committing yourself to a set of guidelines for the rest of your materials and finishes. Of course, rules are made to be broken, but they are also there as a useful guide to the less experienced, helping you create a harmonious interior. Here is a basic guide:

■ **FLORALS AND CHECKS** In pastel shades or traditional hues, these are good for a country-cottage or country-house look. Combine them with pine for a rustic look or darker woods, in conjunction with pastel paints, terracotta, and slate, for a

Formal stripes in rich green set the tone for a Regency townhouse, working well with dark wood furniture and other traditional detailing.

Geometric, bold motifs can be combined with more daring, contemporary finishes.

paper samples

grander effect. Modern florals in a bold palette work well with equally bold paintwork and ceramic tiles, beech or oak, and a touch of glass.

■ **STRIPES** (and other geometric patterns) Wide and bold stripes create a formal traditional town-house look. The colorway influences the mood, but deep greens, golds, and clarets suggest a Victorian or Regency townhouse. Combine with similar tones of paint, mahogany, and encaustic tiles. Narrower stripes suit a country-cottage look, too.

■ **MOTIFS** These change with fashion, and it is not hard to spot the difference between a traditional motif (a fleur de lys) and a contemporary one (an abstract swirl.) Choose your other materials accordingly. For a modern look mix the motif with glass, bleached wood, and a touch of metal; for a traditional motif—look to history books for inspiration—combine it with dark wood paneling, antiques, and velvet cushions edged with gold braid.

brushes

paper samples

ANTIQUING WALLPAPER

In some houses a wall of pristine new paper doesn't look quite right. In period properties especially, brand new wallcoverings are usually a little too bright and a little too perfect for the rest of the room, whereas a wall that looks as if it has survived a generation or two has more character and a softer, more mellow look. It's for this reason that many decorators choose to finish a new wallcovering with a colored glaze. This is a finish for a standard wallpaper rather than a vinyl wallcovering, since the glaze will adhere more effectively to the surface.

INGREDIENTS

- Oil glaze
- Tubes of artist's oil color in raw umber and black
- Large plastic container with lid
- Wooden spoon or stick to mix
- 2 medium-sized soft paintbrushes

METHOD

- Hang the chosen wallpaper on the walls.
- Make up a colored glaze in the plastic container, using the oil glaze, water, and the oil colors. Follow the instructions. Usually the recommended mix is 1 part glaze to 4 parts water—1 gallon (4 liters) of glaze is sufficient to antique 40yds² (40m²) of wallpaper. Mix the oil color—a generous squeeze of burnt sienna with a tiny speck of black—with a little of the oil glaze to thin it, then add some of the color drop by drop into the main glaze

mix. If you find you have added too much color and the glaze is too dark, correct it by adding more diluted glaze until it is paler again. The finished tint should be a couple of tones darker than the base color of the wallpaper.

- Working on a small area at a time, apply the colored glaze with a soft brush so that the area of wallpaper is coated with a thin layer, then brush it off with a dry brush. Work extremely gently—you don't want to saturate the paper, or to brush off the wallpaper pattern with rough strokes. The longer you leave the glaze to dry, the heavier the antique effect will be, so work fast, but in small areas, until you have finished the job.

fabric samples

staples

A FABRIC WALLCOVERING

For a soft, insulating effect, cover the lower part of a room's walls with fabric, above a baseboard and underneath a chair rail. This is quite an advanced project, and it will be necessary to enlist a friend's help.

INGREDIENTS

See first step for all quantities
- *Thin wood battens, measuring 1in x ½in (2.5cm x 1.25cm)*
- *Strong fabric, such as baize or linen*
- *Baseboard*
- *Chair rail*
- *1in (2.5cm) nails*
- *Hammer*
- *Staple gun and staples*

METHOD

■ Measure the circumference of the room, discounting doors and any other "gaps." You need materials as follows: enough wood battening to go around the edge of the room twice—at the top and at the bottom of the fabric—and for vertical supports every yard (meter). Fabric must be at least 48in (1.25m) wide, covering the wall to chair rail height, with enough margin to staple it to the battens. Buy a length equal to the room's circumference, plus an extra yard (meter) to allow for corner tucks. Buy chair rail and baseboard to fit the circumference of the room, discounting any gaps.

■ Nail horizontal battens to the walls so that the top edge of the batten is level with the top of the baseboard when the latter is held against the wall. Fix a second row of battens around the wall at a height of 1yd (90cm) from the floor. Fix vertical battens at 1yd (90cm) intervals between the horizontals.

■ Cut your material into lengths, fitting each length of wall, leaving 2in (5cm) at both ends of each piece to turn in the edges. Start with the shortest length of wall, enlisting a friend to hold the fabric smooth, and working outward from the center. Use the staple gun to staple the fabric to the horizontal battens, keeping it straight top and bottom and placing staples 2in (5cm) apart along the center of each batten. The vertical battens hold the fabric away from the wall, and stop it "bowing." Turn the fabric in neatly at each corner and staple it in place.

■ Once all your fabric panels are stapled in, nail chair rail and baseboard in place. Align them with the edges of the battens to avoid gaps, and nail them through the battens. Paint them to match the fabric.

FINISH	APPLICATIONS
LINING PAPER A base paper for wallpaper or paint	Where walls are uneven, lining paper provides a better surface on which to hang the wallpaper—especially if it is very high quality. Lining paper is hung in the opposite direction to the top paper (i.e. horizontally).
PRINTED WALLPAPER The basic, most common type of wallpaper	This sort of paper offers the widest choice of patterns and colors, but nothing extra in the way of protection. It is often spongeable, so it can withstand light cleaning, but is generally not recommended for heavy-duty areas such as children's rooms and kitchens.
PAPER-BACKED VINYL Wallpaper coated with a film of plastic	The plastic coating on this paper can hardly be seen; it just has more of a sheen than the basic papers. This makes it stronger and more washable so it's a good choice for hallways, children's rooms, bathrooms, and kitchens—especially if condensation is a problem.
SPONGEABLE Wallpaper coated with a thinner plastic film	The thinner protective coating means it is not as durable as vinyl papers, but it can still be wiped with a damp cloth. Use it in light traffic areas, such as bedrooms and dining rooms.
WALLPAPER BORDER A decorative strip, (either self-adhesive or requiring paste)	This is a quick and easy way of adding pattern and creating a theme in a child's room or a bathroom. It draws attention to the proportions of the room so if, for instance, it is positioned at the join between walls and ceilings, or placed at picture-rail height, it will have the effect of lowering the ceiling thus making the room appear smaller.

FINISH	APPLICATIONS
TEXTURED AND EMBOSSED PAPER Heavyweight paper with relief patterns	Ideal for hiding uneven or cracking walls, and also for offering extra protection to walls in heavy traffic areas, such as hallways. A popular application is to use this paper below chair rail height, finished with paint, such as eggshell or vinyl silk, then complement it with wallpaper or paint above the chair rail.
PAPER-BACKED FABRICS Fabrics with a paper backing	A luxurious finish, suitable only for very low traffic areas, such as a guest bedroom or dining room. It creates a very traditional effect. You may need special adhesive for this kind of wall covering and you must take care not to get any paste onto the surface of the fabric.
WOODCHIP PAPER Wallpaper textured with small pieces of wood	A low-cost paper that helps to conceal imperfections on walls and can be painted. In the past it has been a popular choice for hallways. Even the move toward all things textured has failed to make this a fashionable paper though, and it is hard to remove once it is on the walls.

paper renaissance

Wallpaper has made a big comeback. For many years it has taken second place to simple painted surfaces but now is back in fashion, and it's time to relish the instant decoration and texture that wallpaper can provide. It can be used to set the scene or theme within your living area, and, with so many patterns and textures available, you will be spoiled for choice.

tiles

ON WALLS, floors, and even tabletops, tiles are decorative, versatile, and practical—the decorator's ideal finish. Used to cover an entire surface or in isolation as a special feature, tiles offer endless possibilities for introducing color, pattern, and texture both in themselves and in the way you arrange them.

basics

wall tile

natural floor tile

mosaic tiles

Encaustic tiles in traditional patterns make excellent hall floorcoverings that typify Victorian style.

TYPES OF TILE

There are tiles for every sort of surface and finish, which will be looked at in more detail in the rest of the chapter, but essentially you can divide them into four categories:

■ **FLOOR TILES** These may be either ceramic or made from a natural material, such as stone or slate. Those from natural materials are usually square or rectangular in shape, whereas ceramic ones are available in a greater variety of shapes.

■ **WALL TILES** These tiles are usually ceramic. They are available in a number of shapes, although square and rectangular are still the most common.

■ **RELIEF, DADO, AND EDGING TILES** Often raised and curved in shape, these tiles are perfect for finishing and enhancing a tiled area.

■ **MOSAIC TILES** Usually small, these tiles are used in a variety of colors to create a pattern or even a picture.

ARRANGING TILES

The standard pattern for arranging tiles is in blocks, with each tile aligned with the next one, both vertically and horizontally. This is fine, especially if you want a simple contemporary finish or are adding interest with a variety of colors or designs of tile within the layout.

Before you reach for the grout, however, think about the effect of laying your chosen tiles a bit differently. You could try turning them to create a diamond shape or combining different shapes of tile, for example rectangular and square. This does take careful planning, though, to ensure that the tiles fit evenly into the selected area. It is best to position all the tiles first, before you start laying them.

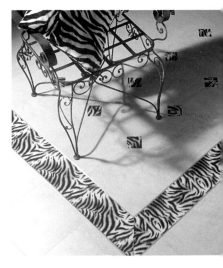

PREPARING THE SURFACE

It's important that the surface to be tiled is smooth, sound, and dry. Any unevenness will be accentuated as soon as you start to lay the tiles, and the adhesive will not work if the surface is defective.

Dare to be bold. Adding decorative inserts can make a tiled floor much more interesting and eye catching.

Never tile over wallpaper, since this means the tiles are essentially being held to the wall by wallpaper paste alone. Similarly, a painted surface will need to be rubbed down with sandpaper to allow the adhesive to penetrate to the wall behind.

If the surface is already tiled and in good condition, you can tile over it—although be careful in a bathroom or kitchen that the extra depth of tiles does not prevent you from turning taps on and off easily. Rub down the existing tiles with silicon carbide paper to provide a key for the adhesive.

MAINTENANCE

Hard tiles can easily be kept looking good with warm water and a mild detergent. However, porous tiles such as terracotta, quarry, and encaustic need to be sealed to prevent them from staining. Always mop up any spills as quickly as possible, and use a little ammonia to lift stubborn marks. Generally the grout is harder to maintain. It can be cleaned with tile-grout bleach (available from the supermarket).

natural floor tiles

stone tiles

For neutral, natural flooring, nothing beats stone and terracotta. The natural world offers an unimaginable range of colors, patterns, and textures so no two tiles will ever be alike, and the effect is always timeless. Tiles are also the easiest and cheapest way of laying a stone floor, since they are lighter and thinner than slabs or flags. Tiles may be machine- or handmade, glazed or unglazed, inlaid or plain. The disadvantages of tiles are that they can be cold, noisy, and slippery when wet—and anything you drop on the floor is likely to break.

Basically the tiles you choose will depend on your budget and the color and texture you want. Here is a rundown of the most popular types:

■ **TERRACOTTA** Made from fired earth, these tiles come in a variety of colors from brick red to flinty gray. They are available in different shapes and sizes, with machine-made ones looking rather crisper than handmade ones. They retain heat, so are warmer than other tiles, but are porous so they need sealing.

■ **GRANITE** This stone is exceptionally hard wearing and impervious to water. The colors of granite range from near black through to mottled

Simple terracotta flagstones are practical and effective in large hallways and kitchens.

white, with a flecked surface. It can be rather slippery, especially if polished.

■ **LIMESTONE** Cool, elegant, and softer than granite, limestone is porous (but it can be treated to prevent staining) and has a light tone, ranging from beige to gray, with a mottled surface.

■ **SANDSTONE** A warm reddish stone, sandstone is also porous and stains easily but is cheaper than limestone. Yorkstone, a form of sandstone, is harder wearing and non-slip.

■ **MARBLE** This stone simply cries out "luxury." It is sophisticated and cool, but very expensive. The influx of cheap imitations has meant it can also verge on the vulgar if used in the wrong setting.

Even the most contemporary interiors can combine practicality with style when it comes to flooring.

■ **SLATE** The colors range from deep green and blue to purple and black. It is cheaper than granite or marble, waterproof, hard wearing, and low maintenance, but the darker shades do show scratches.

The natural beauty of stone adds pattern, color, and detail to any room.

■ **QUARRY TILES** These tiles are a mass-produced alternative to terracotta tiles, although they are colder underfoot. They come in a variety of shapes and sizes, but square is standard. Reminiscent of Victorian kitchens and halls, the tiles are available in shades of buff, brown, and red. They are hard wearing and reasonably non-slip, although they mark over time.

ceramic tiles

ceramic floor tiles

You can give a room instant character by finishing the floor with a certain pattern or color of tiles. The way you finish the floor has as much impact on a room as the color or finish you give to the walls, so make your decision carefully.

Because ceramic tiles can be made with such a crisp, clean edge, they are ideal in a contemporary setting, where an even, regular finish is required. They come in a fantastic range of colors—from the most earthy and subtle to the boldest and brightest of shades—and a variety of shapes, patterns, and even textures. For an older home, such as a Victorian house, encaustic tiles—available in a range of traditional patterns and colors—are the perfect finish for a hallway or kitchen. It is not always neces-

With the laurel leaf-patterned curtain and elegant Roman bust, classical black and white tiles are the perfect choice for this traditional bathroom.

sary to seek out something new and fashionable. In both the traditional and the contemporary home, few things have as much impact as a shiny white ceramic floor or one laid in the classic white and black checkerboard design. White tiles, however, do show the dirt more than those in other colors, so need constant cleaning.

Ceramic floor tiles resist water and most stains, which makes them a good choice for bathroom and kitchen

floors as well as utility areas. The downside is that it is tiring if you have to stand on ceramic floor tiles for a long time, they can be cold and slippery, and your favorite perfume bottle will be smashed to smithereens if you drop it. Sometimes, too, if you drop a heavier item the tile itself may break.

When you are choosing ceramic floor tiles, don't forget to pay some attention to the borders of the room. Border tiles are useful for adding definition and giving a finished look, and, in a modern open-plan house, they can be used to define one area as being separate from another. In any home, an irregularly shaped room, with chimney pieces and alcoves to work around, can be given a sense of order if the border tiles are set in from the edges enough to create a more regular, even outline.

ceramic edging tiles

ceramic wall tiles

ceramic wall tiles

Ground, refined clay is pressed into molds and fired at a high temperature to make ceramic wall tiles. They can then be machine glazed, embossed, and decorated with a relief design, or hand-painted for a more individual finish.

As a wall finish, tiles do not have to be used only in areas where they are required to cover a substantial area. Instead treat them as much as a decorative finish as a practical one (some hand-painted designs are works of art in their own right), and use them to make a frame around a window or alcove, or even fix some special tiles on a wall as you would a group of small pictures. This is a great way of incorporating expensive tiles into a scheme when you can't afford to use them all over a wall.

Alternatively, you can mix and match expensive designs and cheaper basic tiles the same size as the special ones. Cover the wall mainly in the budget option, slotting in the more expensive ones for an individual finish.

To emphasize the rustic nature of handmade ceramic tiles, lay them wider apart, with up to ⅕in (5mm) between them. For a sleeker contemporary look, position the tiles close together when laying them, using tile spacers to make the job easier.

A mix of brightly colored wall tiles is a great way of adding pattern and color to an otherwise practical room.

contrasting tiles

Border tiles are just as important on a wall as they are on a floor. An expanse of tiling looks more finished when it is edged with a decorative tiled border. Border tiles are basically rectangular and come in a variety of designs, such as rope, rail, or "plain slip." A chair or edging rail is a must if you are only tiling the lower half of the wall to chair rail height, unless of course you are going to finish it with a wooden molding instead.

Where wall tiles meet the edge of a bath, sink, or other fixture, use ceramic coving and fix it with a flexible sealant to make a waterproof seal.

Tiles laid in a diamond pattern behind the sink lift the whole bathroom and provide a contrast with the more standard tile arrangement on the wall.

patterned and relief tiles

relief pattern tile

Adding pattern to a tiled area can help to define the theme or style of a room, in the same way as a patterned wallpaper will anchor a room's look in a particular era, country, or movement. The pattern you choose will dictate the mood, be it florals for a relaxed country home, geometric shapes for a more formal effect, the free-flowing lines of Art Nouveau, or a contemporary pattern such as circles and spots.

Some designs in particular are extremely evocative of a certain time or place. Traditional blue and white stylized floral tiles are reminiscent of French, Italian, or Spanish homes, with their cool hallways and sun-filled rooms, whereas more somber-toned encaustic tiles with heraldic and geometric motifs are reminiscent of the Victorian home (although, historically, they go back as far as or further than medieval times and can also be seen in many old churches and religious buildings).

Whatever pattern you choose, bear in mind the scale of the area you are finishing before you commit yourself. Patterned tiles are best used as insets at intervals or to decorate a block within some plainer tiles. In

Traditional patterns immediately give the floor the feel of a particular era, thus setting the scene for the rest of the decoration.

By choosing a tile with a certain motif you can help create a theme within a room.

general, the busier the pattern, the smaller the area it should cover. Many tile retailers have a service to help you plan a tiled area successfully, but if you haven't been offered this, turn to pages 118–119 for more help.

Complete pictorial panels made up of tiles can make a dramatic statement. They work especially well in alcoves and small rooms, or when used to define areas, such as behind the stove in a kitchen. You need to choose the theme of the picture with care—it is likely to be with you a long time.

For those who are nervous about introducing a pattern, one-color relief tiles are a compromise. They have a raised pattern in the same color as the rest of the tile, creating a change in pattern and texture, without introducing too obvious a design.

mosaic

broken tiles for mosaic

Mosaics offer pattern and color variation in a subtle yet striking way and bring life to any surface. At its simplest, a mosaic pattern is an ad hoc mix of tiny, different-colored tiles. However, in the hands of a professional, such patterns can become works of art.

Usually the use of mosaic tiles is limited to small areas, partly because of the time required to lay so many tiles over a large area, but also because they can in fact look more effective as a border or panel—perhaps as a backsplash or baseboard. The bonus of mosaic tiles is that they can be used on curves and will fit irregular shapes better than conventional tiles.

Bits of broken pottery or ceramic tiles make ideal pieces to use as the basis for designing your own mosaic.

Mosaic tiles are generally made from small cubes of marble, stone, terracotta, or unglazed ceramic—or a mixture. Squares are most common, but you also find rectangular, hexagonal, and round mosaic tiles. Just like other hard floor tiles, mosaic can be cold, but as more grout is required than in other tile finishes, the overall effect is a little less slippery.

The combined weight of mosaic tiles is considerable, so for flooring it is best to lay them on a concrete sub-floor. If you are determined to lay the

You can take your inspiration from ancient Roman mosaic designs or be even bolder and create a striking pattern all of your own.

tiles on wooden floorboards, put down a sheet of plywood first to create a stable surface.

To facilitate fixing, some manufacturers now produce sheets of tiles. The chips are held together either on a netting backing that is applied to the wall or on a layer of removable paper that is soaked with water and peeled off once the tiles are laid.

OTHER MOSAIC SURFACES

There is no need to restrict yourself to traditional applications of mosaic. Why not use it to finish the worktop around a sink, a coffee table, or a flat-topped stool? For a unique effect, smash up old ceramic pottery from a second-hand shop (see the project on pp. 120–121 for inspiration).

manufactured mosaic tiles

shapes, colors, and patterns

bright colored tiles

If you want to achieve a beautifully tiled wall or floor using an imaginative selection of colored and patterned tiles, you will need to do a lot of planning. First of all decide on the sort of look you are after. In the same way as you might decide on a look for your entire room, the best way of doing this is to browse through interiors magazines, catalogs, and even history books to see what sort of designs appeal to you.

When you find a combination you like, analyze it. What is it that appeals to you? Is it the way the tiles have been positioned? Is it the type of motif on the tile? You might be able to find a similar tile in the shops, so see if your tile supplier can help.

A small, detailed tile, inserted at intervals, breaks up the expanse of floor tiles, adding pattern and interest.

There is no shame in taking inspiration from other people's work. Just ensure that your idea works with the colors in the rest of the room. If you have a patterned fabric in the room already, try to use similarly toned colors for the tiles. A neutral-colored stone or slate tiled floor will work with most colors, but other tiles should echo or complement wall and fabric colors.

The next step is to find samples of suitable tiles and start creating your

A classic, and with good reason. A black-and-white tiled floor never fails to make a dramatic statement. Choose a tile size to suit the scale of the room for maximum impact.

own design. Measure the area to be tiled and the tile samples you have. Then make a scale drawing of a tiling plan and experiment until you find something you are happy with. Using colored pens to replicate the color of the tiles may help. If you want to create little blocks of patterns with a group of tiles, measure out life-size or scaled-down tiles on the paper and copy the color or design of the tiles on to them so you can try different patterns. Finally, order more tiles than you will need (around 5 percent of the total) to allow for breakages when trimming them to fit—and play around again with the real thing.

Instead of simply mixing tile designs, why not mix your materials too? This floor design combines strips of wood with metal treadplate tiles.

natural stone

combining

So you've set your heart on a certain type of tile—here are some tips on how you can design the rest of the room around it.

■ **NATURAL STONE** This is a designer's dream, although it tends to come at a designer price, too. Natural materials such as stone work well in almost any setting. Combine stone with a cool contemporary interior—bleached wood, glass, metal, and muted paint colors—or think along the lines of Arts and Crafts or of Tudor banqueting halls and start ordering dark woods, rich fabrics, pewter, and wall hangings.

■ **TERRACOTTA TILES** Go rustic or Mediterranean with these tiles. All you need are color- or white-washed walls, simple wooden or metal furniture, few or very simple fabrics, and some earthenware pots.

■ **ENCAUSTIC FLOOR TILES** A Victorian look is an obvious route to take, but if William Morris wall coverings are too fussy for you, approach the design with more restraint. In a hallway, encaustic floor tiles can be combined with ceramic wall tiles to chair rail height and a softer paint color above. Dark wood will complement the earthy colors of the tiles, and stained glass will finish a front door to perfection.

■ **PLAIN WHITE FLOOR TILES** These can look stunning in almost any setting. In a contemporary living room, keep your use of fabric simple and focus instead on beautiful pieces of furniture, metal, untreated wood.

dado tile

Tiling topped with a chair rail-style edging tile adjoins an upper area of wallpaper, creating a finish that is practical but pretty for a hall, bathroom, or kitchen.

In a hallway, add some black, perhaps edging the floor with a black and white border tile in a scrolling or geometric design, and keep the whole style sophisticated with large mirrors and even a touch of marble.

■ **BRIGHT CERAMIC WALL TILES** Although small in area, a kitchen or bathroom backsplash of bright jewel-colored tiles can enliven and complete a scheme, bringing together the various colors in a room in a joyful pattern. Combine it with painted woodwork, bare wood flooring, and painted walls.

■ **MOSAIC TILES** An age-old floor and wallcovering, mosaics have appeared with many finishes over the years. The 21st-century approach is to use them with chrome, colored glass, and pale woods and to treat them as a decorative detail rather than the main element.

Natural stone tiling needn't be confined to rustic schemes. Here warm wood and flooring work effectively in a room that is sleek and modern, with just a hint of the country.

Tiles can be used to make an attractive tabletop.

ceramic floor tiles

A PATTERNED TILE BORDER

You can transform a room by adding a patterned border around a plain tiled floor. This is the most challenging project in the book—if you have never tiled before, turn to the following pages for a simpler option!

INGREDIENTS

- ■ *Tiles for main area and border*
- ■ *Chalk*
- ■ *Two softwood battens*
- ■ *Tile cutter*
- ■ *Plastic tile spacers*
- ■ *Tile adhesive*
- ■ *Grout*
- ■ *Notched and smooth spreaders*

METHOD

■ To lay a tile floor with a border, you must work outward from the center of the room, as with a plain floor. If your room is not square, widths of less than a tile must be made up with tile pieces between border and wall. This space must be allowed for in your calculations. Make a floor plan of the room on graph paper.

■ Choose appropriate tiles for both the center and border of the room, then fill in the floor plan in detail, working from the center and calculating how many tiles you will need, and, if necessary, the width of the gap between border and wall. Allow an additional quantity of 5% when you buy your tiles, to allow for breakages.

■ Nail two battens together to create a right angle using a spirit level. Measure two opposite walls to their midpoints, then draw a chalk line on the floor joining them. Repeat with other two walls, so a chalk cross marks the room into quarters. Loose lay your tiles outward from the center, working evenly, a few tiles at a time in each quarter. As you start a new row, lay your right angle against the edge of the last row to check you are working in straight lines. At the edge of the last row of complete tiles, lay your border. There will be an even gap round the edge of the room into which you will fit your final row of cut pieces. Cut the tiles and lay them in place.

■ When all the tiles are laid, cement them, working from the center, a few tiles at a time, spreading adhesive with a notched spreader. Use tile spacers between them.

■ When all the tiles are in place, leave to dry. The next day, remove the spacers and grout the tiles with the smooth spreader. Leave to dry for an hour, then wipe away surplus grout with a damp sponge.

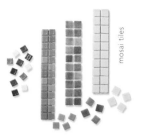

mosai tiles

A MOSAIC MIRROR

With the advent of ready-made mosaic tile combinations available on sheets it has become easy to use mosaic mixes, but it's almost as simple— and more satisfying—to create your own unique pattern.

INGREDIENTS

- *Flat-edged mirror frame made from pine or MDF*
- *Large sheets of cardboard*
- *Scotch tape*
- *Colored pencils*
- *Ruler*
- *Mosaic tiles*
- *Small plastic spacers*
- *Tile glue*
- *Tile cement or grout*
- *Damp sponge*
- *Soft, dry cloth*

METHOD

■ First choose the size of mosaic tiles you want. These will dictate the width of the frame. It should be generous enough to allow you to plan a pattern, and have a good smooth surface. We used a frame four tile-widths wide, plus an additional ⅜in (1cm) to allow for spacers and grouting. Your local frame shop should have a ready-made frame that will fit the requirements. It must be sturdy enough to support both the weight of the tiles and that of the mirrored glass when hung.

■ Create a same-size paper pattern of your frame with cardboard (you can tape sheets together if you don't have a single sheet large enough), then measure the number of tiles you will need and draw a square grid over it.

■ Plan your design with colored pencils so that you know how many tiles of each color to buy.

■ Buy the tiles and arrange them over the pattern on the paper "frame." Then cover the front surface of the real frame completely with about ⅛in (3mm) of tile glue, and, taking one tile off the paper pattern at a time, arrange the tiles on the frame following the pattern, using small spacers to ensure a consistent gap for the grouting. Leave the glue to dry.

■ Remove the spacers and completely cover the patterned frame surface with tile grouting (white or colored, whichever you prefer), being sure to fill in all the corners and gaps.

■ Leave the grout to dry for about half an hour before removing the excess with a damp sponge. Finally, polish the tiles with a dry cloth.

FINISH	APPLICATIONS
CERAMIC TILES Tiles made from fired clay and glazed in a variety of colors	Suitable for walls and floors, but if you are choosing tiles for flooring, ensure that the ones you buy are strong enough for floor use. These tiles can be cold and slippery underfoot when wet, but are otherwise a practical and attractive finish for kitchens and bathrooms.
MOSAIC Patterned tiling made up of tiny pieces of colored glass, tiling, or stone	Colorful and very much in vogue, mosaic tiles are an attractive finish for anything from tabletops and backsplashes to shower stalls and small floor areas. The only practical point to consider is that there is inevitably a lot of grouting to keep clean to prevent it from discoloring and harboring germs.
TERRACOTTA FLOOR TILES Made from fired earth	Available in a variety of shapes and sizes, these can be machine or handmade, with colors varying from brick red to flinty gray. They retain heat, so are warmer than other tiles, but are porous so they need to be sealed. They are well suited to flooring in kitchens, especially in traditional country homes.
LIMESTONE FLOOR TILES Light-toned tiles ranging from beige to gray, with a mottled surface. Portland Stone is a variety of limestone	Cool and elegant, limestone suits both traditional and contemporary interiors, and look especially impressive in large tiled areas. It is porous and needs to be treated to prevent it staining.

FINISH	APPLICATIONS
SANDSTONE FLOOR TILES A warm reddish stone. Yorkstone is a form of sandstone.	Hardwearing and with a nonslip surface, sandstone looks effective in rustic, country-style kitchens and hallways. It is porous and stains easily, but is cheaper than limestone.
MARBLE TILES Expensive, veined stone in shades ranging from cream to gray	Sophisticated, elegant, and cool, marble looks effective as a floor tile in expansive hallways and can be complemented in bathrooms by marble-topped bathroom fittings. It becomes very slippery when wet.
SLATE FLOOR TILES A dark tile with colors ranging from deep green and blue to purple and black	Less expensive than granite or marble, slate is waterproof, hardwearing, and low maintenance, although the darker shades do show scratches. It looks effective in both traditional and contemporary kitchens. The blue/gray colors combine particularly well with glass, chrome, and stainless steel.
QUARRY TILES A mass-produced alternative to the handmade terracotta tile	Popular colors are earthy shades of buff, brown, and red, which suit the colors of traditionally styled kitchens. They are hardwearing, non-slip, and are a practical choice for kitchens, although they will become marked over time.

practicality

Consider how you can use tiles imaginatively and creatively around your home. Their combination of durability, practicality, and good looks makes them a material to exploit to the full. From kitchen worktops and bathroom walls to decorative mosaic patterns and patterned floors, there are tiles available to suit everyone's taste.

wood

NATURAL, simple, and warm, wood is a timeless material that looks as effective in the starkest contemporary interior as it does in the traditional country home. Use it, enjoy it, and watch it grow even more beautiful as the years go by.

basics

Wood, in its many shapes and forms, has enduring appeal as a domestic material, and it's not hard to understand why. Used over large areas, such as on a floor, it not only looks beautiful in its own right but also acts as a foil to the other finishes and furnishings

The knots, grain, and warm color of wood have a pattern and detail that man-made surfaces simply cannot replicate. It also comes to look even better as it ages.

in the room, somehow allowing them space to shine and be appreciated in a way that most carpets and other floor coverings do not.

No doubt one of the reasons that wood has remained so popular is that it is derived from a living source. The naturalness of the material allows it to combine effortlessly with man-made finishes, and the almost infinite variety of patterns and colors makes it a more interesting finish that domi-

Covering walls with wood paneling immediately adds character and a traditional style to any room.

nates its surface area less than a machine-produced material, making it easier to live with.

Wood is already well established as an ideal finish for floors, window frames, and doors, but don't ignore its potential as a wall or ceiling finish, or as a work surface in a kitchen or study, too. When considering wood for an interior, be aware that you don't have to use it in its natural or varnished state. Wood takes stains, paint, and other decorations well and can easily be adapted to blend with your other fixtures and furnishings.

Wood works as effectively in a contemporary interior, combined with glass and chrome, as it does in a more traditional one, combined with brass hardware and sash windows.

nails

THE CHOICE

Because wood has been used and appreciated in the home for so long, many different forms or applications of wood have been developed and come in and out of fashion over the years. Not only are there dozens of different types of wood to choose from (*see pp. 128–129*), but you can also now buy wood in a variety of forms— strips, sheets, blocks, boards, mosaic tiles, and parquet. You also have the choice of buying newly cut wood from a merchant or splurging on instant character and going to an architectural salvage yard for old, reclaimed wood.

MAINTENANCE

It is precisely the natural qualities of wood that make it such a good investment. While most man-made surfaces deteriorate over time, wood ages with style, and any knocks only add to its charm. Wood is susceptible to changes in humidity, however, so it is not recommended for wet, steamy areas, such as bathrooms, unless they are well ventilated. Protect floors from stiletto heels and grit and, every few years, resand and varnish the surface.

types of wood

Capitalize on the many varieties of wood that are available. Whether you want a pale fresh finish or a deep, dark effect, there is a wood that will fit the bill. Make sure, however, that the wood you choose has been grown in a renewable estate and has not been cut from an irreplaceable rainforest or indigenous woodland. Only buy imported tropical timber if it is certified by a body such as the Forest Stewardship Council or Rainforest Alliance's SmartWood group.

Bleached and limed woods create a simple look and avoid the stronger orange tones of pinewood.

Wood works well in modern decorative schemes, adding warmth to a room of exposed brickwork, glass tables, and chrome fixtures.

In addition to the color, the strength or pattern of the wood may also feature in your choice. The part of the timber you buy and the way it has been cut all affect its density and grain. The toughest is end grain, for example, and the next hardest is quarter sawn, whereby the wood is cut radially, producing a more even grain pattern. Plain sawn timber,

beech

teak

maple

yellow pine

oak

especially softwood, has lots of knots and wears less well, but it is cheap and easy to obtain.

Here are some of the more common varieties of wood from which you may choose:

■ **PINE** A pale softwood that turns golden yellow when sealed with varnish. It is very economical, but less durable than other wood types.

■ **OAK** A favorite flooring timber. The color varies according to the variety (American, English, or French), and the grain is coarse. It is very hard-wearing and will resist rot.

■ **MAHOGANY** An endangered tropical hardwood, so buy it with caution. It has a deep brown color and has been popular for furniture and doors.

■ **ELM** A rich and dark-colored wood that resists water and is very strong.

■ **MAPLE** A wood with a golden red tinge and open grain. It is good for flooring, since it is tough enough to withstand heavy wear and tear and does not "squeak" underfoot.

■ **BEECH** Pale with a fine texture and grain. It is often used for woodblock flooring.

■ **ASH** Pale with a straight-lined grain and a coarse texture.

See the applications chart (p. 146) for more details on how these woods can be used. It is also worth asking a reliable lumberyard for details on the individual strength, defects, fire grading, and resistance to worm or fungi, since qualities can vary, even from batch to batch of the same timber.

other forms of wood

Laminated flooring is composed of a base of softwood or a composite wood, a thin veneer of hardwood, and a laminated protective surface. Its tongue and groove structure makes it easy to slot pieces together.

Because wood has become so popular and supplies of timber are not inexhaustible, there has been an added incentive over the years to produce man-made or "adapted" wood. After all, if you are planning to paint the wooden surface, you don't need the real thing below. And if you are planning a state of the art interior, why not take the theme of function and utility one step further and opt for a plywood rather than a solid wood floor? Apart from anything else, it will save you a lot of money.

PLYWOOD

Forget any conceptions of plywood being flimsy or makeshift—it is now seriously chic. Made from lots of thin pieces of wood (usually birch) glued together at right angles, plywood is unexpectedly strong—especially if made from solid birch. It comes in panels in thicknesses of up to ¾in (20mm) and can be cut into squares and tongue and grooved to make it easy to lay as a floor or as wall paneling. Once laid, it can be sanded lightly and varnished to give it shine and warmth, or you can paint or stain it. The downside of plywood is that it is not that long lasting, but its low cost more than makes up for this.

Painting effects a complete transformation of basic wood finishes such as plywood or MDF.

MEDIUM DENSITY FIBREBOARD

Commonly know as MDF, this board has been crowned king of materials by numerous DIY programs on TV. It's cheap, easy to cut and shape (always wear a dust mask when doing so) and very smooth. MDF is sold in panels of various sizes and is good for anything from kitchen unit doors and wall panels to screens and bath panels.

The perfectly smooth surface of MDF makes it ideal for finishing with paint and other effects, as long as it is primed first with MDF primer or a mixture of paint and bonding agent.

VENEERS

Veneered, laminated woods are a cheaper way of achieving the effect of solid wood flooring. A thin layer of hardwood is fixed over a softwood or composite wood base and laminated to protect the wood. The boards don't need varnishing—because of the laminate—but they cannot be refreshed by sanding, so the laminate needs to be effective.

Laminated flooring looks sleek and modern. The only downside is that it can't be resanded in the way that a solid wood floor can.

light wood panels

light woods

Pale and beautiful, the lighter woods create a look which is fresh and contemporary and works especially well with the pale and neutral palette of modern interiors. Pale wood is often associated with Scandinavian style, but whether it is used on work surfaces or as shelving, on stairway treads or to cover an entire floor, pale wood provides a warmth and pattern to interior surfaces that might otherwise feel cold or bland. If you want a simple or utilitarian look, you may simply appreciate pale wood's subtle patterning and color in its own right as it can add a quality to a room that no man-made finish can provide.

NEW WOOD

To achieve a pale wood effect, you will either need to lime or bleach existing woodwork or floorboards (see p.139), or invest in new pale wood such as beech, ash, or pale oak. Pine is also a pale wood in its natural state, but when it is varnished it becomes quite orange in color and is imbued with a rich tone. Oak in particular makes a fantastic surface, but it can be expensive. If you are looking for a slightly less costly material, try press-dried beech, which is actually harder

Extend your use of wood to built-in wooden furniture to create a uniform, streamlined look. Here a wooden cabin bed and built-in closets in the same wood make the most of available space in a loft conversion while creating an uncluttered effect.

than oak, but less expensive. Generally, the larger the dimensions of the strips, the more they will cost, but wider boards do look more luxurious.

Solid hardwood flooring and worktops are expensive and are best fitted by a professional. Afterward you will need to protect the surface in some way—especially if it is going to be used as flooring. Some strip flooring comes treated with an acrylic hardener, otherwise you will need to seal and protect it yourself with a few coats of varnish (see p. 138).

Even pale wood can provide warmth and pattern. Here a cool, contemporary hallway is transformed by the texture, color, and grain of the wood, and the contrast of the wood against the pale walls helps highlight the dramatic staircase.

dark wood

dark wood panels

Dark woods evoke a sense of grandeur reminiscent of a traditional country manor. Wood paneling on the walls, stripped wooden floorboards, exposed beams on the ceiling, and solid, dark wood furniture create a look that offers an instant sense of history.

RESTORING OLD WOOD

There is nothing more satisfying than lifting the corner of an old carpet and discovering fine solid floorboards below. Most wooden floorboards in 19th- and 20th-century houses are pine, laid horizontally across the floor. Being a softwood, pine has the advantage of being easy to sand. Don't worry if pine is paler than the look you want to achieve as it is easy to buy and apply colored wood stains and varnishes that will darken the wood to a color you are happy with. In older properties you may find oak boards in wider planks, or even mahogany in narrow strips. Either way, in just a few days you can sand, color, and varnish old boards to create a floor that looks great and will work with any style of interior, traditional or contemporary. Restored wooden floorboards are also practical as they are able to withstand a lot of wear and tear.

If you prefer something more unusual and individual than simple

Often the pattern, color, and detail provided by the wood in a room is all that is needed to decorate it. Here the exposed beams suit the age and size of the property but avoid adding such details to your own home unless they are appropriate to its age and scale.

floorboards, then why not consider parquetry (blocks of wood arranged in geometric patterns) or marquetry (wood inlaid with contrasting blocks of wood)? Both of these techniques were popular as long ago as the 17th century, but they still look good in most interiors, and particularly good in dark-colored woods. You could adopt the Victorian approach and use parquetry or marquetry as a border around the edge of a floor only, perhaps placing a rug or carpet in the center. Parquetry and marquetry are also cost-effective ways of incorporating into your home certain woods that would be too expensive to use over a large area, such as walnut and American cherry.

Wood wall paneling creates a cozy, warm feel and is ideal for hiding less than perfect walls underneath. You do, of course, lose a certain amount of space in the room, and it can make the space feel rather dark, so this sort of paneling is best used in rooms where light is not an issue.

preparing wood

If you want to make the most of existing wood in your home, it's likely that you will need to update or repair its finish in some way. Perhaps you want to give it a coat of paint, a stain, or a fresh coat of varnish, or maybe you want to tackle one of the projects in this chapter—either way you will need to prepare the wood first.

Above and below: Before you can refurbish and decorate an old wood floor, it will need to be sanded and maybe stripped of any old paint or varnish. If you are painting the entire floor, a light hand sanding may suffice—for other fiinishes you may need to use an industrial sanding machine.

Even brand new wood needs some attention and preparation. All wood needs to be seasoned before it can be laid. This basically means allowing it to acclimatize to the level of humidity and the temperature of the room in which it is to be laid. Newly cut wood generally shrinks once it comes into a heated room and loses some of its natural moisture, so it needs time to do so before it is restricted by fixing. Most good manufacturers will only supply wood that is ready to lay—and some will guarantee that it is fully seasoned.

Old wood will need to be sanded at the very least; it may also need to be stripped of paint or old varnish before use, which requires considerable physical effort. If you are tackling a moveable piece of furniture or a door and do not like the idea of getting to work with chemical stripper and tools yourself, try looking for a local firm who will dip the wood for you.

Large areas, such as floors, generally need to be sanded by machine, unless the floor is already very even or you are going to paint it with a special floor paint, in which case you may get away with giving it a light rub -down by hand. Usually, though, it's best to rent an industrial floor sander. If the floor has been painted you need to remove most of the paint with a heat stripper and scraper first or the paint will clog up the sandpaper. Then knock down any protruding nails and remove any staples or they will rip the sanding sheets, wasting time and money. If you are at all nervous about doing it, call in a professional—or a friend who has done it a few times already!

Newly laid wood will need to be protected with several coats of varnish. Choose a gloss varnish for a high shine finish, or satin for a more matte effect.

After sanding save a little of the sawdust and mix it with wood glue or wood filler to obtain a firm consistency. Use this mixure to fill any small gaps between the boards. It will make the finish better, and cut down on drafts.

decorating and finishing wood

varnish

When it comes to finishing a wood surface, you need to decide whether you want to enhance the natural beauty of the wood or use it as a blank canvas on which you can create your own patterns and add your own colors. If you fall into the first camp, then you should look at finishes that will allow the grain and perhaps also the color of the wood to be appreciated, such as varnish, light stains, washes, and liming. Otherwise, you can take full advantage of any paints and stains that appeal to you and be as creative as you dare.

VARNISH

A coat of varnish will allow you to fully appreciate the grain and color of wood—although, be warned, it does tend to make pine develop rather orange tones. Most varnishes will yellow and darken the wood a little, but much less than they used to; acrylic floor varnish, however, does not yellow. The choice of sheen is up to you—gloss can look a little too shiny, but if matte looks too dull to you, you could try a mid-sheen finish. Gloss varnish is harder, but it is slower to dry. Try to give a floor a minimum three coats, but five is better if it will need to withstand much traffic.

Newly sanded, pine floorboards look quite pale, but once they have been varnished they develop a warm, golden shine.

LIGHTENING WOOD

To prevent pine taking on an orange hue under a coat of varnish, you could try lightening the wood first to produce a paler, more Swedish, look. Brushing bleach on to the wood will take all the color out of it (experiment with a small area first to see if it has the effect you are after), so for a more subtle effect you can buy white-pigmented varnish

or a wood wash, but these can be rather expensive. Another alternative is to lime the wood by painting white paint, liming wax, or gesso into the grain of the wood then rubbing it "off" and into the grain with a rag. Repeat the process until, finally, you have a film of pale color all over the wood.

Bleaching wood gives it a well-worn, almost weatherbeaten look, which can work beautifully with a pale color scheme.

DARKENING WOOD

If you prefer the more dramatic shades of mahogany, but are faced with a floor of pine, you can use special wood stains to achieve the depth of color you are after. Wood stains also come into their own if you have to lay a few new floorboards and want to age them a little to match the others before varnishing.

Wood stains are an economical way of transforming the look of the wood you have in your home.

combining

For a fresh, modern room, combine new woods with pale, subtle paint colors.

Even wood paneling can look contemporary when it has been given a coat of cool-colored eggshell paint.

Designers love wood because, being a natural material, it works so well with almost any other finish. That said, certain colors and patterns of wood (even the patterns suggested by the length and direction of a room's floorboards) inevitably suggest a certain look or mood that is particularly appropriate to one or two styles. So, if you have to work around an existing wood floor, you might want to bear in mind the following suggestions:

■ **VARNISHED PINE OR OAK FLOORBOARDS** These classics of wood flooring have been particularly popular for the past 20 or so years. Today a room of varnished floorboards still suggests warmth and character, but we have moved away from the trend of faithfully restoring every period detail in our old homes to the extent that, while we still appreciate the beauty and practicality of the stripped wood floor, we are happy to combine it with anything from shabby country chic to glass walls and aqua paint—it works with everything.

■ **PLYWOOD AND MDF** Used as varnished panels on the walls or on the floor, these provide a modern finish for those with simplicity and utility in mind. They should be combined with concealed storage, glass shelves, tones of white paint on the walls, and, ideally, a Le Corbusier chair or two. With painted plywood and MDF, though, you can soften the effect to achieve almost any look you desire.

■ **PAINTED FLOORS** A plain painted floor can work well in anything from a stark contemporary interior (especially if it is painted in white or black) to a country-cottage bedroom, if combined with gingham and florals.

Similarly, limed floors work well in both rustic and town houses, but colored washes and stenciling are suggestive of more decorative styles such as American Folk Art (blood red and green) or rural Scandinavia (pale blues, soft grays, and mint greens).

A painted floor creates a homespun traditional effect combined with wooden furniture and wicker chairs.

Giving wood a wash of translucent paint allows the grain to be appreciated through the color.

■ **TONGUE-AND-GROOVE PANELING** The most universal wooden wall treatment of all, pine tongue-and-groove boards work best when they are painted in an oil-based paint or colorwashed to allow the grain to be seen. (If you are surrounded by varnished tongue-and-groove you soon feel as if you are in a sauna.) Often used in bathrooms to chair rail height, this paneling works well with other bleached woods and materials such as coconut-fiber matting, stone, and plaster.

brushes

oil paint

A DECORATIVE STENCILED FLOOR BORDER

Wooden floorboards look great painted, stained, or colorwashed, and a stencil border can be surprisingly effective. You can create as contemporary or classical a pattern as you wish. Here, we finished a floor with a crisp, geometric stenciled design for a modern look.

INGREDIENTS

- ■ *Sandpaper*
- ■ *Wood filler*
- ■ *Paint or wood stain*
- ■ *Cardboard or thin board*
- ■ *Clear acetate sheet*
- ■ *Scalpel*
- ■ *Cutting board*
- ■ *Floor paint for stencil*
- ■ *Masking tape*
- ■ *Medium paintbrush*
- ■ *Small paintbrush*
- ■ *Matte or gloss floor varnish*

METHOD

■ Prepare your floorboards carefully—remove any protruding nails, sand them lightly, and fill any gaps with wood filler.

■ Paint or stain the boards with your base color, following the manufacturer's instructions, and leave to dry.

■ Make your stencil by drawing a simple geometric pattern, like the one shown opposite, onto cardboard and trace it on to an acetate sheet. Then lay the acetate over the paper on a cutting board and cut the stencil out with a scalpel. Trim any ragged edges.

■ Measure the placement of the stencil carefully, working out the number of repeats and marking them on the floor with chalk to ensure you have left space for complete patterns. Measure inward from the baseboard regularly, also, so that the stenciled line is a consistent distance from the wall. When you've outlined the complete stencil area with chalk guides, stick the stencil in position on a corner with masking tape and carefully fill it in using a medium paintbrush and your chosen color of floor paint.

■ When the stencil is filled in, remove the masking tape, lift the stencil, wipe it free of any surplus paint, and reposition it for the next repeat. The outer line shown opposite was simply achieved by painting between two straight lines of masking tape to add extra emphasis to the border.

■ When you have completed the stencil border, leave it to dry. Finish the floor with a coat of matte or gloss floor varnish for extra protection.

tongue-and-groove lengths

TONGUE-AND-GROOVE PANELING

This is one of the most impressive yet simple effects with wood. You can now buy packs of ready-cut lengths of tongue-and-groove paneling that simply slot into place and, if you invest in some panel glue, you won't even need to use a hammer and nails to fix it!

INGREDIENTS
- *Tongue-and-groove lengths*
- *Baseboard*
- *Chair rail*
(See below for quantities)
- *Spirit level*
- *Pencil*
- *Panel adhesive*
- *Matte oil paint to finish*

METHOD
■ Remove any existing baseboard. Measure the circumference of the room, allowing for any gaps left by doors, cupboards, windows, and so on. Measure the height you want your chair rail to be, which will give you the correct length for your tongue-and-groove pieces. Ask the lumberyard to give you the correct number of tongue-and-groove lengths (or packs) to fill the space, and buy enough chair rail and baseboard lengths to finish.

■ Using a spirit level, draw a light pencil line around the room to mark the top of the paneling.

■ Traditionally, the wood strips were

slotted together and invisibly nailed on to battens fixed to the wall. Today you can buy strong panel adhesive to do the job for you, allowing you to fix the tongue-and-groove straight to the wall. Slot together a strip at a time, running a little glue along each edge as you go and following the adhesive manufacturer's instructions. Keep checking the vertical and horizontal lines with a spirit level.

■ Use the same adhesive to fix the chair rail and baseboard at the top and base, covering the rough ends and making a neat finish.

■ Stain or paint the tongue-and-groove paneling to complement your color scheme. Here, we finished it with two coats of matte oil paint in a vibrant orange.

FINISH	APPLICATIONS
TONGUE-AND-GROOVE PANELING Traditional wooden wall treatment	Good for disguising poor walls, or covering old tiles, pine tongue-and-groove boards can be varnished, painted in an oil-based paint, or colorwashed, which will allow the grain to be seen. It creates a traditional, beach-cottage look suitable for informal rooms and bathrooms. This paneling works well with natural materials such as coconut-fiber matting, stone, and plaster.
PLYWOOD Thin layers of wood glued together under pressure to create a strong structural board	For a cheap utilitarian finish, plywood can be used as varnished or painted panels on walls or floors—otherwise its use is limited to basic structural applications.
MEDIUM DENSITY FIBREBOARD (MDF) A man-made variation of wood	The beauty of MDF is that it can be cut easily with a jigsaw to any shape (wear a mask while you cut), it doesn't need sanding, and is very smooth for painting. This has made it a popular choice for furniture, closet doors, screens, shutters, table tops, etc. Paint it first with a sealing coat of MDF primer (available from DIY stores), or a mixture of five parts of your finishing paint and one part wood glue.
PINE FLOORBOARDS	A traditional flooring, especially popular in old town and country houses. Sanded, maybe stained or bleached, and then varnished, pine floorboards offer a practical, hardwearing, and long-lasting surface that will improve with age. Combine with rugs for added warmth and comfort.

FINISH	APPLICATIONS
MARQUETRY A pattern of inlaid veneers of wood, fitted together to make a design	A popular finish on furniture, but also used to create attractive designs either in the center or around the edge of a wood floor. It is a cost-effective way of incorporating woods that would be too expensive to use over a large area, such as walnut and American cherry.
PARQUETRY A floor covering comprised of pieces of hardwood, fitted together in a decorative fashion	Like marquetry, parquetry is more usually associated with furniture, but it makes a beautiful patterned wood floor. Waxed to bring out the natural colors of the wood, it is particularly reminiscent of grand Georgian interiors, but also of Art Deco design. Use it in hallways, living rooms (with rugs), and dining rooms.
NEW WOOD FLOORING Usually solid pine, beech, ash, or pale oak	Laying new wood flooring allows you to obtain a smoother, tighter finish than original floorboards can offer. This sort of flooring suits almost any interior, but is especially appropriate in modern spaces. It needs to be sanded and varnished once it has been laid, but can be periodically resanded and finished to renew its good looks, making it a lasting, beautiful surface.
LAMINATED WOOD Plywood, topped with a thin veneer of natural wood and sealed with a laminate for protection	A cheaper alternative to solid wood flooring. The advantage of good laminated flooring is that it can be remarkably resistant to stains, heel marks, and cigarette burns; its disadvantage is that it can't be resanded once it is damaged. It is well suited to modern homes in living rooms, dining rooms, and bedrooms. Most laminates are not suitable for bathrooms, or other areas where they may get very wet and suffer extremes of temperature.

adaptability

Whether it's man-made, veneer, or solid, wood is sure to play a part in your design scheme in some shape or form. Painted, varnished, bleached, stained, or left in its natural form, wood is a forgiving material which will allow you to adapt its looks to suit your changing needs. Perhaps best of all, wood is one of the few surfaces that can actually improve with age.

glass &
metal

FRAGILE, but strong, opaque, and transparent, glass
is a material of contradictions, yet it is these
paradoxes that make it such a versatile, useful, and
beautiful material for the designer to employ. Metal,
too, is something of a paradox, with some metals,
such as copper, being used to add a touch of luxury,
while others, such as steel, convey a hardworking,
utilitarian quality.

glass: the basics

Stained glass can turn a window into a work of art.

If you are thinking of making use of glass in any unusual way in an interior, always consult an expert before you start. Glass can be beautiful, space enhancing, and chic, but in isolation it is a dead material. It may have been shaped or cut into the most imaginative forms, but by itself it has no value. However, the combination of glass, the right structure and setting, and appropriate lighting can provide more interest than any opaque walls and decoration can offer. Creating a living space with large expanses of glass, whether in windows, doors, or walls, allows you to use the light you have to the maximum, creating changing moods.

There are many varieties of glass products, all offering a different style, function, or mood. But every one is made from the same basic materials— only the composition, thickness, and coatings have been adapted to help it fulfill a specific purpose.

Using glass as a structural material allows you to create practical room dividers with a greater impression of light and space than solid walls.

■ PRIVACY AND DECORATION

If you want a glass that will obscure or conceal the view of what lies behind it, then look for one that has been acid etched, sandblasted, or colored, either partially or completely. These processes are also used purely to make glass more attractive. Other options for decorative features are to have a shaped glass window between rooms, a curved, bevelled-edged glass room divider, or leaded glass windows.

■ SOLAR AND THERMAL

CONTROL Some types of glass have a special composition or coating to offer a certain level of heat and light transmission—great for saving energy and reducing heating costs.

If you can't stretch to the expense of glass walls, ceilings, or floors, use glass to finish a tabletop, creating a sleek, contemporary surface.

■ **NOISE CONTROL** Specially thick glass, insulating units (such as double glazing), laminated glass, and high-performance acoustic laminates all cut the amount of noise that passes through the glass—an essential consideration for glass-paneled walls.

■ **SAFETY AND SECURITY** Glass can be toughened or laminated to make it safer in case of breakage (a must if there are children around).

■ **MECHANICAL STRENGTH** Glass used to build stairs or a ceiling needs to be especially strong. Certain glasses are adapted for these purposes.

MAINTENANCE

Glass is best kept clean by washing it with hot water and detergent, or with a glass-cleaning material. Allow glass flooring to dry thoroughly before anyone walks on it, since it can be very slippery. Glass ceilings are more difficult to keep clean because they are less accessible. In addition, the glass may have to be load bearing to facilitate cleaning. Your architect will advise you.

glass blocks

glass blocks and sheets

Many people today live in homes that are made up of one or two multifunctional spaces where members of the household gather to talk, relax, watch television, read, or study—and even cook and eat. One space now needs to perform a different role for different family members at different times.

This is where glass blocks and panels as room dividers or screens come into their own, allowing you to define part of a room for a specific purpose, without creating a solid wall and losing the impression of space or light. They are also the perfect solution if you have considered knocking through into another room or corridor to introduce more natural light, but are nervous about the loss of a certain amount of privacy or wall area.

Glass blocks are the perfect material for separating two areas without losing the impression of space or light.

Glass blocks can offer the practical benefits of a standard plain wall, but also make a strong, individual impression. They can be built to your specification—filling a space from floor to ceiling or simply to waist height—while also adding an element of interest. The choice of glass blocks today is very wide, with designs incorporating different patterns, textures, shapes and even colors. The type of finish—textured or patterned—will affect the opacity of the glass, and perhaps influ-

Large windows help to bring the outside in, allowing you to extend your perception of the room's size, and of course, appreciate the view.

A glass stairway is the ultimate way to make a fashion statement.

ence the style of the room. Think about whether you would like what lies behind the glass to be visible, distorted, or completely obscured.

GLASS FLOORING

The ultimate in dramatic flooring, yet, paradoxically, the most invisible too, glass floors and stairs look amazing when well lit. Always take professional advice about which type of glass to use. Two possibilities are thick annealed glass, which is heated and gradually cooled to add strength, and float glass, which takes its name from the way it is hardened. All glass floors should be sandblasted in strips to make them less slippery.

mirror tiles

mirrored glass

The ubiquitous sliding mirrored closet doors of years gone by have a lot to answer for—not least because they succeeded in turning a whole generation away from mirrored glass as a finish. In fact, mirrored glass has a lot to offer. Add a sheet of mirrored glass to a room in the right context and it can do wonders for the space, making it appear larger, lighter, and more vibrant. Mirrored glass was being used to enhance interiors as early as the 19th century. Then, architects would fix a large sheet of mirrored glass to an alcove to create a false window or archway, thereby fostering the perception that the room stretched further than it did.

Combining glass of different types will create a light and dramatic space, confusing the perception of a room's actual boundaries.

The power of mirrored glass can still be harnessed in the same way—only with a contemporary twist. The light-reflecting qualities of mirrored glass are the perfect complement to today's wealth of shimmering, silver-embossed fabrics, metallic paints, and touches of chrome. Use wall-sized mirrored sheets to extend a small hall, kitchen, bathroom, or shower room; fix a sheet of mirrored glass behind display shelving in an alcove; or, for a slightly more traditional effect, frame oversized mirrors that stretch almost from floor to ceiling in a chunky wooden or gilt frame and fix one—or two— behind a dining table to reflect the candlelight. Ensure that whatever you place in front of the glass is worth seeing twice. The reflected image is as important as your choice of artwork or decoration. Ensure that you use lighting that will add sparkle, not a blinding glare, once it is reflected.

MIRRORED TILES

These can look wonderful but should be used sparingly. Small mirror mosaic tiles can be fixed imaginatively as a chair rail–style decoration around a room or used to bring a dull closet front or coffee table to life. Larger mirrored tiles can also be used in small areas to create an Art Deco effect. You cannot rely on mirrored tiles to increase the impression of space, but with good lighting they can really come to life.

Covering a large expanse of a small bathroom wall with mirrored glass serves to visually lengthen the room.

colored glass

Color adds a further decorative dimension to glass, turning the white light which passes through it into glorious colored rays.

Elaborate stained-glass windows are beautiful—but are best left to the professionals. They make a striking impression, but are very costly to create.

Traditionally, colored glass is associated with the stained-glass windows of Gothic or Victorian interiors, or perhaps the ubiquitous Art Deco sunrise motif that graces so many bay windows in homes of the 1930s. Today you can use colored glass in many more creative ways, thanks to an increase in the variety of colored glass products available.

Glass blocks come in a wealth of colors, all of which can create an effect quite different from that achieved with the more standard clear varieties. With colored glass you can create different patterns within a panel of glass blocks, complement or continue the other colors in a room's scheme, and create patterns elsewhere in the room with the light that shines through the blocks to make pools of color on the walls and floor beyond. Colorless glass blocks distort the image of what lies beyond anyway, but colored blocks add another element, offering more intrigue.

Stained glass can make a feature or focal point out of a central or very small window, or perhaps a glazed door. It is an ideal way of reinforcing a theme, too—in a nautical-style bathroom, for instance, why not commission a

Houses built in the 1930s often feature bright and bold stained glass, helping to counter the plain and simple style of Art Deco interiors.

stained-glass window in a fish, dolphin, boat, or mermaid design? A local glass supplier will usually be able to recommend a stained-glass artist to work with you—or may be able to undertake a simple, geometric design themselves. You don't have to commit yourself to an entire window of color if you are nervous about its impact or expense—you can choose to have only a small panel at the top of the window colored.

If your budget or your confidence doesn't extend to replacing an entire window, or you feel creative, you can dabble with color by painting a pane of glass yourself with special paints. For a temporary approach, fix sheets of colored acetate over some panes and see the difference it makes.

Make the most of a small window by turning it into a colored feature.

metal: the basics

Few budgets stretch to using solid gold or silver, so instead the more basic metals are polished, cast, and shaped to create decorative finishes. If you want a material that is durable, but can also offer shimmer and luster, you need look no further than metals. They provide many of the reflective, light-enhancing qualities of glass, but in a more subtle way.

copper

More and more people have come to recognize the raw beauty of metal in its most practical forms. You can now see converted warehouse "luxury" apartments with their large structural steel girders stretching, totally exposed, across the main living area.

brushed metal tile

The key to success is to use metal in a way that will complement and enhance its surroundings. Metals can all be finished or applied in such a variety of ways that there is one to suit every sort of home. The most common finishes are polishing or burnishing (for a less glossy sheen); they can also be etched or sandblasted for texture, and hammered to produce a pattern or texture. It is also possible to paint metals, for example old kitchen cabinets, but they need to be primed first to provide a key for the paint.

plain metal grid

Some of the more commonly used metals are:

■ **COPPER** A rich-looking non-magnetic metal that is reddish brown and bright when polished, but develops a green patina if it is allowed to tarnish. It is often used as a base for metal plating, such as chrome and silver. Sheet copper can be used effectively to face worktops.

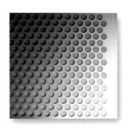

patterned sheet

Clean, shiny metal is hygienic, so is well suited to kitchens and bathrooms. Splashes of color can prevent the overall look becoming too sterile.

■ **BRASS** This metal is a mixture of copper and zinc, the proportions of which change the color from light yellow to dark gold. It is most often used for decorative details, such as door hardware.

■ **ALUMINUM** Silvery in color, soft, light, and non-magnetic, aluminum has a wide range of applications, including Venetian blinds and rolling shutters.

■ **STAINLESS STEEL** A strong, shiny, tough, and malleable metal, which comes in a variety of sizes of sheets and is good for wall finishes and kitchen fixtures.

■ **GALVANIZED STEEL** This is steel or iron that has been coated with zinc to prevent it from rusting if left outside.

MAINTENANCE

Special creams are available to keep stainless steel and other metals looking shiny and new. They are simply applied then rubbed off with a soft cloth (always follow the manufacturer's instructions). For larger surfaces, such as metal floors, washing with hot water and a little detergent is effective.

textured metal samples

metal walls and doors

As more and more homes are converted from semi-industrial buildings, metal is becoming a popular finish. Exposed steel girders and fire-escape stairs are common in warehouse and loft apartments, so turning to metal for other surfaces is an obvious choice. Metal is most often used in thin sheets, covering a base of another material, such as a wooden countertop or a plastered wall. A touch of chrome, stainless steel, or aluminum will give your decor a real edge. Here are some ways you might consider incorporating metal surfaces in your home:

METAL BACKSPLASHES

Fitting a sheet of stainless steel behind your countertops makes a refreshing change from the more traditional tiled backsplashes and gives your kitchen a modern, professional touch. Stainless steel's highly polished surface is good for reflecting light back into the room and requires little maintenance—just a polish with a special cleaning fluid now and then. Obviously this design only works if your kitchen units are sleek and contemporary looking, too—it's not a finish to mix with cottage-style cabinets.

Brushed stainless steel tiles provide a professional-looking backsplash that goes well with other stainless steel appliances in the kitchen.

Practical and chic, metal countertops and walls create a very contemporary finish that will come to life under artificial lighting, too.

METAL PANELING

If you are feeling bold, you can make a real impact by covering an entire wall with stainless steel panels. One wall behind a dining table could be covered with three or more large panels to shimmer and reflect the candlelight at night, or choose a wall opposite a window in a living room and enjoy watching the different subtle light changes and reflections on its surface.

Manufacturers have responded to demand and are producing stainless steel doors on their appliances to suit the thoroughly modern kitchen.

SLIDING PANELS/DOORS

One way of creating a truly industrial finish is to cover a sliding door panel with a sheet of stainless steel or aluminum. This gives an air of solidity to a door (although aluminum itself is quite light) and looks most effective in a small kitchen or bathroom where the fixtures and trim are largely chrome or stainless steel as well.

metal floors and fittings

metal door handle

FLOORINGS

Metal flooring—usually aluminum or galvanized steel—is the height of industrial chic, looking bold, shiny, and very modern. The advantage of aluminum is that it is so much lighter than steel, which could be useful if you are laying it over a timber floor, and it doesn't rust, making it a better choice for damp areas. You will have the choice of sheet metal or tiles, depending on the effect you want to achieve. Sheets need to be cut to size and pierced with holes so that they can be screwed in place. Both should be finished with some sort of textured raised pattern, such as the treadplate designs shown opposite, to make them less slippery. The downside of metal, apart from the cost, is that it is cold and noisy underfoot.

FIXTURES

Kitchens and bathrooms are good places in which to experiment with metal. Units look smooth and sleek fronted with stainless steel and, ideally, should be finished with an equally contemporary handle or an invisible push-open magnetic catch. And, since you can buy a good

Illustrating that metal flooring needn't be dull or unattractive, metal treadplate tiles are here combined with other tiles to give a practical, non-slip surface in the areas that need it most, while producing an effective flooring design.

textured floor samples

range of stainless steel appliances, there's no need to interrupt the line with, say, a white-fronted dishwasher. Countertops, too, can benefit from a stainless steel surface. It will be hygienic and easy to keep clean, and the way in which the metal bounces back the rays of light from any light fixtures above really brings a room to life.

Once seen only in professional, commercial kitchens, stainless steel appliances have made their way into the modern home.

If you are worried that an all-metal look will be too clinical, soften the overall effect by combining the metal surfaces with some wood or glass-fronted units, too (see p161). Finish them with a chrome handle or knob to maintain the metal theme.

METAL CEILING SUPPORTS

If you have a large open-plan area with columns acting as ceiling supports or decoration, consider facing them with chrome or stainless steel sheet for a glamorous hi-tech look.

textured flooring design

combining

Metal and glass surfaces are the in thing in contemporary design. Both are very much at home in the modern interior, working well together and in isolation. But they both have their place in more traditionally designed homes, too—just choose a finish or application to suit your scheme.

Used in practical areas such as the kitchen or bathroom, metal and glass come into their own. For a minimalist look, combine simple metal industrial units with stone or metal flooring and exposed brickwork, or perhaps a textured paint finish. White is an obvious paint color to choose, but prevent the room from feeling too clinical by treating a wall or cupboard front to a brighter splash of color. A warm, traditional look is achieved by using copper and brass. The project on pages 166–7 shows you how to rejuvenate an old unit with sheet copper.

Glass partition walls need to be combined with sleek surfaces to complement their 21st-century design.

Glass blocks work well in kitchens and bathrooms, but they can sit comfortably in less functional parts of the home, too. Use glass blocks to create a full or half-height divider between a living room and dining area, or between a kitchen and sitting/dining area. The floor surface should be hard (carpet would look wrong), but you can achieve warm tones by using wood or colored linoleum. If you choose colored glass blocks, keep the walls subtly colored, or even white, to allow the filtered light to provide the decoration in the room. A glass-topped dining table or glass shelving will continue the look throughout the room.

In a more traditional home, use stained glass to provide decoration. You might think a suitable location would be a Victorian hallway, but stained glass will work with most styles. If you live in a period home, look in books for inspiration and, if possible, use the colored glass as a starting point for the rest of the color scheme. You needn't feel too bound by tradition—take inspiration from the fact that Chichester Cathedral, built in the 11th century, is graced by stained-glass windows by 20th-century artist Marc Chagall.

When glass meets stainless steel the effect is light, bright, and thoroughly modern.

A room featuring a lot of glass and metal sometimes needs extra warmth and pattern. Try adding the natural color and grain of wood.

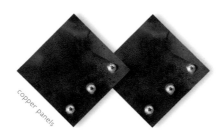

copper panels

A COPPER-PANELED CUPBOARD

Turn old or flat-pack furniture into something more original with a copper-paneled door. A distressed sheet of copper is fixed to the wooden door with brass tacks to create a truly individual piece.

INGREDIENTS

- ■ *Small cupboard with flat wooden door*
- ■ *Thin copper sheet, cut to fit the door exactly*
- ■ *Spray mister*
- ■ *Box of kitchen salt*
- ■ *Protective gloves*
- ■ *Mask*
- ■ *Blow torch*
- ■ *Brass upholstery tacks*
- ■ *Small-headed hammer*
- ■ *Small brass door knob*

METHOD

■ Measure the cupboard door carefully. Take the dimensions to a metal supplier and ask them to cut a piece of thin copper sheeting exactly to fit. Explain what it is for, so they can help you choose the weight—it must be thin enough to hammer through, but thick enough not to warp when you use the blow torch.

■ You can either ask the supplier to torch the panel or do it yourself. If you opt for the latter, do the work in a large clear area on a cement floor, work at arm's length, and wear protective clothing,

gloves, and a mask. Lay the metal flat on some bricks to raise it off the floor slightly. Hold the blow torch at a distance of 12ins (30cms) from the metal and begin to heat the surface. Work in short bursts, turning the torch away while you mist the metal and sprinkle salt every minute or so. This helps to give some patination to the finish, so it does not have to be done evenly, but you must be extremely cautious as the water will spit when it comes into contact with the hot metal. Direct the blow torch onto the metal for short periods only—if it becomes overheated, the sheet will warp.

■ When you are happy with the range of color and patina you have, turn off the blow torch and leave the metal to cool completely. Then polish the surface with a soft dry cloth to reveal the finish.

■ Fix the panel to the cupboard door with evenly spaced brass upholstery tacks. To finish, add a brass door knob.

masking film

stencil design

ETCHED-GLASS CUPBOARD DOORS

Spray-etching glass is a great way to add pattern and interest. Whether it is the glass in your bathroom window, the glass panel of a door, or, as here, a glass-fronted cupboard, you can quickly transform the surface with just a can of etching spray and a stencil.

INGREDIENTS

- Small cupboard with clear glass panel or panels in the door
- Tracing paper
- Pencil
- Scalpel
- Cutting board
- Clear masking sheet
- Lightweight spray adhesive
- Masking tape
- Can of etching spray
- Protective mask

METHOD

■ First choose your pattern. For the doors opposite, we used a real leaf, pressed flat and outlined on tracing paper, but you may want to use a pattern from a book or magazine, or a creation you've drawn yourself. It should have a reasonably simple outline, so that it is possible to trace and cut.

■ Lay the tracing paper outline on a cutting board, under the masking sheet. Then cut carefully through the sheet round the outline of the shape with a scalpel to make your stencil. Neatly trim any ragged edges.

■ Cover the wood around the glass with masking tape to protect it from the spray adhesive and the etching spray. Then use the lightweight adhesive to fix the stencil to the glass panel. Wear a protective mask over your nose and mouth while spraying. Make sure the edges of the stencil are flat against the glass surface so that the etching spray cannot bleed underneath and spoil the pattern.

■ Following the manufacturer's instructions on the can, spray smoothly and evenly on the stencil, trying to cover the area without stopping, so as to avoid making lines and breaks in the finish. In this instance, a single coat will look better than two.

■ Leave for five minutes, then gently remove the stencil and the masking tape. If you have more than one glass panel, tackle them one at a time.

FINISH	APPLICATIONS
MIRRORED GLASS	Sheets of mirrored glass help to reflect light and give the impression of space, as well as being practical in a bedroom or bathroom. Use mirrored glass to cover entire walls or alcoves to trick the eye into believing there is further space beyond.
MIRROR TILES Tiles of mirrored glass	Their popularity has declined slightly, but under artificial light they can come to life so could be useful in a room with little or no natural light. They can also add a period feel to a specific style of interior, for example, used with loud 1970s' style wallpaper.
GLASS BLOCKS Bricks of glass in a variety of colors and degrees of translucency	These can be used singly to create a "window" in a solid wall, or to build a wall to separate two areas without reducing the amount of light or the impression of space. Colored blocks cast patterns of colored light into a room when artificial light or sunlight shines through them
GLASS SHEETS Glass cut to size, available in a wide variety of colors, degrees of translucency, and strengths	Sheet glass can be adapted during the manufacturing process to suit almost any application, from windows and ceilings, to flooring and partition walls. You should always consult an architect, structural engineer, or specialist glass supplier for advice on the type of glass most suitable for your chosen application.

FINISH	APPLICATIONS
GLASS FLOORING	Only consider if you are working with an architect or interior designer, who can get you the technical help you will need. Very costly; used in contemporary interiors to create the impression of a space without floors, walls, or doors, in conjunction with glass partition walls and ceilings. Thick annealed float glass is commonly used, and needs to be given a non-slip treatment, such as etching, to make it safe.
COLORED GLASS Glass colored or stained in the production process	Effective in large or small feature windows, either divided into areas of pattern and different colors with leading or simply used as a single sheet of color. Walls of colored glass blocks equally can be made up of more than one color of brick to create a multicolored room divide, or made entirely of one color.
SHEET METAL Sheets of metal such as stainless steel or copper, cut to size and available in a variety of gauges or thicknesses	Once cut by a professional, this can be used on walls, backsplashes, cupboard fronts, and worktops. Most suitable for the kitchen, creating a semi-industrial finish.
METAL FLOORING Metal tiles with a textured surface	The overall effect is practical and industrial, so it is best used in working areas, such as kitchens and bathrooms. To soften the look, you could combine metal treadplate tiles with another material, such as ceramic or linoleum.

futuristic

These are the materials of the future. As manufacturing processes develop and improve, glass and metals will become stronger, more adaptable, and have even more applications than before. Glass walls and ceilings, currently used only in designer homes, could soon become the norm, blurring the boundaries between indoors and out.

putting it all together

YOU have mastered the basics of color theory and paint effects, and been inspired by the range of surfaces and finishes that are now available, but applying all of this to your own home can still seem a little daunting. This section of the book allows you to see how all the different finishes can work in particular rooms and gives you plenty of tips on putting your scheme together.

textures

No matter how much you spend on fabrics, paint, wallpaper, and fittings, your room will feel and look somewhat dull if it lacks textural contrast. "Texture" has become something of a buzz word with designers, but combining textures successfully in the home has always been part of good interior design. The skill lies in effectively mixing and matching different materials (fabrics, surfaces, and furniture) so that the overall effect is varied yet complementary. It sounds easy, and really it is, but still people make the mistake of creating a room that is one-dimensional—made up of all things cotton and smooth, or all things shiny and hard.

Add texture to walls to give an additional element to your design. Here the relief pattern on the chimney piece echoes the pattern on the mantelpiece below.

The pattern on the cupboard doors is reinforced by that of the fruit bowl, giving a unified look.

Consider how different materials make you feel when you touch or see them. Velvets, furs, wools, and chenilles are appreciated for their warmth and softness; metals and glass for their light-enhancing qualities; and wood and stone for their unique natural beauty. A room that contains elements of all of these will appeal to the senses of sight and touch, and will allow you to feel more able to relax and be "at home."

So, if you desire a rustic-style bedroom with stone walls and a wooden floor, finish it with something softer—a length of voile, a

woollen rug, or tactile bed linen—to give the space more balance. A room with a neutral color scheme particularly needs the variety of tone, grain, and texture that a combination of materials provides to compensate for the uniformity of color on the walls and in the furnishings.

Even the most simple modern designs will benefit from an awareness of the different effects achieved by mixing elements of warm and cool, matte and shiny. Yes, employ the contemporary essentials of glass and metal as extensively as you like, but remember to add warmth with some touches of natural wood, too. The room will gain balance and the final result will be easier to live with.

Voile draped over a bed can imbue a modern room with a touch of romanticism.

This industrial-style stairway is made more appealing in a domestic setting by combining the steel and etched glass with the warm, mellow tones of wood.

upholstery

Your upholstery can dictate or reinforce your room's style or theme. Here animal prints suit the scale of the room and its furniture, and are the perfect complement to the collection of masks.

Lengths of pink curtaining instantly transform this room into a soft-looking space, casting warm shadows inward.

In most homes it is the upholstery that adds the color and pattern, and stamps a style on a room. This is exactly what makes so many people nervous when it comes to committing themselves to a final choice, because they realize that their selection makes a statement about their character and taste, and feel reluctant to "expose" themselves if they lack confidence in this area. There's no need to feel this way—experiment with a cushion or a throw before settling on fabric for a sofa or drapes to ensure you can live with a color or pattern.

Think about your furnishings—rugs, drapes, and upholstery fabrics—in the same way as you considered your wall surfaces, and turn back to the pages on color theory (see *pp. 20–25*) and using

Mixing patterns is always more effective than slavishly repeating the same pattern throughout. Here florals and stripes combine to create a scheme that looks as if it has evolved rather than having been consciously designed.

patterns (see pp. 86–93) for reassurance and guidance. Patterns on fabric will be perceived in the same way as patterns on wallpaper. A large-scale pattern will dominate a small area, making a grand statement, and a small-scale pattern will be lost when used over a wide area, such as on a set of floor-length drapes covering a large feature window. So ensure that the pattern you choose suits not only the size of the room but also the scale of the piece it will cover, be it a window, sofa, or bed.

By contrasting colors and mixing patterns you can use upholstery to create a homey, welcoming room. Choose colors and patterns to follow one style, whether it is traditional, ethnic, or contemporary.

If you are uncertain which colors to opt for when it comes to choosing a fabric, take inspiration from one of the pieces you know you have to work around. Unless you are lucky enough to be starting from scratch, you are likely to have a sofa, carpet, or set of drapes that will need to be a part of the new scheme. Pick out the dominant color from these and then look either to contrast or to harmonize with it by referring back to the color wheel on page 24. A blue sofa, for instance, can be the starting point for many different looks—combine it with blues and lilacs for a cool harmonizing scheme; opt for a brighter finish by contrasting it with bright yellows or orange; or go for classic blue and white, especially in a sunny room.

Build up confidence in your ability to mix and match patterns, as well as colors. A room can look a little sterile if each element in the room is plain, whereas it can be overwhelming if every piece features the same design. Again, the trick lies in recognizing the scale and density of patterns, then mixing them to create a balanced effect. For example, to mix florals and stripes, take a bold-patterned floral fabric, perhaps with a plain, open (so less dense) background, and mix it with a boldly striped fabric in one of the colors featured in the floral design. Then mix these with a small-scale print in the same or a harmonizing color. Use a color wheel to help you if necessary (see pp. 24–25).

To create a contemporary look use upholstery with restraint, opting for simple blinds or panels of fabric, rather than elaborate drape treatments.

choosing a style

Traditional red walls and an ornate bed frame are teamed with a modern chair and picture, giving a balanced look of old and new.

Here, a mix of finishes has resulted in a comfortably eclectic interior.

Living in your home for a few months before making any major decorating decisions is always a good idea. Get a feel for the place and how you live in the space before calling in decorators or knocking down walls.

When it comes to choosing a style for your home, the best advice is to be led by the architecture of the house itself. You don't need to follow the details of a previous period's style slavishly, but an attempt to create "warehouse minimalism" in a Victorian terraced house is unlikely to work easily. Think also about the needs of anyone sharing the house with you. Will Victorian paraphernalia be

practical for two toddlers and a dog, for example, or will the elderly appreciate the stark nature of very modern living spaces?

If you live in a period home, it is worth doing some research into that era to see how it might have been decorated then. Not only is it an interesting exercise, but it can unearth some surprises. A house

built in the 1890s, for example, may not have been decorated in the high Victorian style of dark colors, heavy drapes, and plenty of clutter. Art Nouveau was emerging then, demanding light-filled rooms and simple, well-designed furniture—which might appeal more to contemporary tastes.

Be sympathetic to the space you live in, and let it guide you in your choice of style.

The contemporary, clean lines of this furniture are perfect for this large modern living space.

The neutral tones of the furniture are modern and chic, but it is the key accessories and splashes of color that really bring this room to life.

If your home's history (or lack of it) offers little inspiration, look to other eras, countries, or styles instead. Today's multicultural diversity offers a wealth of inspiration, but the trick is to mix old and new, without creating a message that is too confused. Choose key pieces of furniture from one style or theme, then you can develop your own look with a mixture of accessories that complement the room. Don't be too led by fashion—style will last far longer. Nor do you have to re-create a look faithfully. Instead take the elements that appeal to you and be creative. It does help, however, to have some basic knowledge of various different styles.

STYLES TO RESEARCH

■ **16TH AND 17TH CENTURIES**: wood and tapestry dominated.

■ **18TH CENTURY—GEORGIAN AND COLONIAL**: elegant, symmetrical style; Gustavian elegant painted woods, pale palette; late 18th-century Shaker style of simple, practical honest furniture, homespun fabrics, quilts, tongue-and-groove paneling.

■ **19TH CENTURY—VICTORIAN**: dark colored, excessively decorated.

■ **1890S—ART NOUVEAU**: fresh look with an emphasis on craftsmanship.

The simple, elegant ornaments and subtle lighting make this hallway appear spacious while remaining warm and inviting.

■ **1920–1940—ART DECO**: Hollywood movie style with chrome and lacquer.

■ **ORIENTAL**: Simple, low-level furniture, ebony, lacquer, and bamboo.

■ **ETHNIC**: Terracotta, rattan, tin, textiles, and batik.

While the walls are filled with pictures, the furniture remains plain so that the overall look of this room isn't too cluttered.

living room walls

The living room is the multipurpose space where the family comes together to watch television, listen to music, study, and chat. It is somewhere you relax in the evenings and perhaps play by day.

If you mostly use the room at night, create a warm, relaxing environment that looks good in artificial light and by candlelight. Orange, terracotta, and shades of red and golden yellow are ideal colors for painted or wallpapered walls, but exposed wood or brickwork looks great, too, especially when lit to highlight its ruggedness. If you use the room more by day, you may prefer a fresher, lighter finish.

With the growing trend for open-plan, multipurpose living spaces, your living room may also double

wall-covering samples

The pattern created by bare bricks is in complete contrast to that provided by a classical wallpaper, but both are effective in their own right.

up as your dining room, kitchen—and maybe even your bedroom—so go for a color that will suit all these areas. A neutral scheme works well. Screens may usefully act as moving walls in these situations. Choose solid wood or fabric-covered screens for complete division, or try a translucent glass screen to create a sense of separation from the rest of the room, while maintaining the feeling of space and allowing daylight to flood in.

Open-plan living has created a demand for moving walls or screens that offer a flexible approach to room dividing.

living room floors

natural stones

Comfort or aesthetics—the choice is yours, but the two can be made compatible.

Your choice of flooring for the living room will come down to your lifestyle and preference. Should you choose the natural, hard-wearing beauty of polished wood, go for the softer, more comfortable option of luxurious wool carpet, or perhaps pick the middle ground and choose a natural fiber floor-covering such as sisal or coconut-fiber matting?

Carpet, particularly in the form of wall-to-wall carpeting, has declined in popularity in recent years, as people have moved generally toward simple, cleaner lines. The shift to open-plan, multipurpose living areas has played its part here, too, since a hard, practical floor surface, such as wood or

Natural floorings, such as coconut-fiber matting, offer durability and can be more comfortable underfoot than bare wood.

Natural wood flooring retains a natural warmth. Of course rugs can always be added to a room if the weather gets really cold.

linoleum, is as attractive in the living area as it is effective in the kitchen and dining areas.

A compromise that works well in both traditional and contemporary style homes is to go for a combination of wood flooring and rugs. This offers the beauty of wood, but the warmth of something softer underfoot where you need it.

Natural floor coverings are a good alternative, especially for people who find it hard to decide on a color for carpeting. Sisal, coconut-fiber matting, and seagrass offer a natural style in subtle color schemes that will work with any decoration, in the same way as wood. They wear well too, but they stain quite easily and can be hard to keep clean.

stainless steel taps

kitchen features

The style of your kitchen will be dictated by the material, color, and finish of the cabinets and countertops as they cover so much of the surface area. If you are investing in new units, do plenty of research before you buy. The kitchen is essentially a working space and the surfaces need to be hard-wearing and practical. But the kitchen is often also the social heart of the home, where everyone congregates and visitors are entertained, so you don't want to create an overly clinical environment.

Again, you need to be aware of your own needs. If you would rather not spend all day polishing and cleaning, then steer clear of white or metal countertops, glass-fronted cabinets and tables, and any other surface that will show every mark or smear.

Kitchen units cover so much of your wall surface, they will inevitably determine the style of the room.

Tiled countertops are easy to wipe and clean. Laminated countertops are a good budget option and can withstand hot pans and sharp knives. Stone, such as granite, marble, and slate, creates a more luxurious finish, and does not have to be prohibitively expensive—if it is cut thin and finished with a double depth at the edge to create the illusion of depth.

Wood makes an attractive surface for countertops and units in modern and traditional kitchens, but it is softer than tiles or laminates so you need to take care with knives and hot dishes. Darker woods and pine are great for a country look, painted wood can create an American Shaker effect, and light woods such as beech or maple combine with glass, chrome, and stainless steel for a modern finish.

Wooden countertops are attractive but harder to keep in pristine condition than laminates or tone composites.

electric kettle

kitchen floors & tiles

Kitchen flooring needs to be practical, but that doesn't mean it has to be boring. Far from it. In fact, many people see the open expanse of a kitchen floor as an opportunity to make a dramatic statement, so consider how you might be creative with yours. Even a small floor provides the chance to be creative, and you may even be able to afford more expensive flooring materials than you think you can because you won't need to buy much of them.

Practical needn't be dull. With rubber, metal, linoleum, and vinyl to choose from, you can be more creative than ever before in the kitchen.

The most popular forms of flooring for kitchens are stone tiles, vinyl or linoleum, and wood. It's important to choose one that complements the cabinets, so go for natural stone or terracotta tiles

or stripped wooden floorboards if you have a country-style kitchen, and choose something sleeker to finish a contemporary kitchen. Don't dismiss vinyl—some manufacturers now produce such good quality designs, imitating everything from tiles to wood, that it is hard to differentiate them from the real thing. And linoleum can be professionally cut into individual designs to create stunning flooring.

Backsplashes can be enlivened with a stylish tile treatment. Sheets of small mosaic tiles are a fashionable choice and much easier to lay than individual mosaics. Choosing just one shade of tile can look chic, whereas three complementary colors mixed randomly looks cheerful and is a good way of injecting color into what can be quite a monochrome setting.

Tiles are practical and easy to clean, making them a good choice for kitchen walls.

If your kitchen floor is small, use it to make a statement. You can afford to splurge on something a little more expensive if you don't have a large area to cover.

calming colors

bedroom walls

Your bedroom should be a room to which you can retreat to relax and unwind after a busy day, so it is not the place for stimulating, busy wallcoverings and upholstery. Instead, opt for calming shades, such as neutrals and soft blues, or warming colors, such as pinks and terracottas, perhaps in a subtle color-washed paint effect.

Of course, your bedroom is your personal space, and is perhaps the only room in the house where you can feel completely free to indulge your own design whims and ideas. It is also the room in the home that receives least in the way of heavy traffic so you can afford to be a little more indulgent in your choice of finishes, perhaps choosing a more expensive wall covering than you would do normally, or choosing opulent upholstered furnishings, knowing that they are unlikely to get ruined in a matter of months by artistic toddlers or parked bicycles.

Wallpaper is a good wall covering and if its pattern features two colors or more, it will provide you with an instant palette for your color scheme. It will enable you to pick out a dominant and accent color for your drapes, fur-

This guest room is simple and pretty. Decorating the wall with a panel of fabric that co-ordinates with the bed linen or drapes is an easy way to create a unified look.

nishings, and bed linen. Try to mix and match across different ranges of fabrics and wallpapers rather than opting for the coordinated collections though —they may do the work for you, but the effect is much less satisfying.

If you are considering having built-in closets made, consider the effect their front will have on the room— a whole wall of fitted closets will dominate a room, unless you can paint them in the same color as the walls. Mirrored door fronts will help to increase the impression of light and space, but remember that you will be able to see yourself at every turn.

Use the finishes on your wall surfaces either to make a space feel more intimate, or to open it up.

Mirrored closet doors give the impression that the room is much more spacious than it actually is.

children's bedroom walls

Make use of fun accessories to brighten up a child's room and perhaps give it a theme.

Bright, fun, and stimulating: the decor in a child's bedroom is the total opposite to that of an adult. Children's bedrooms are great fun to decorate as they allow you to indulge the child in yourself. You can have fun with bright color, stencils, and paint effects.

The key to decorating a child's room successfully is to remember that the child will grow up very quickly. Unless you are happy to completely redecorate and refurnish every two years, it is worth trying to take a long-term view and plan carefully. Think which features are likely to remain unchanged for a while. These are likely to be the more expensive items such as the drapes, flooring, and maybe the

Children's rooms are the perfect place to let your imagination and creativity run wild.

wallpaper. These are the pieces that you need to keep as plain as possible so that they will work with any number of decorative schemes in the future. Cartoon drapes may seem a good idea now, but your child may not appreciate them when he or she is older. Lampshades and pillow covers, however, are relatively cheap pieces to change, so if you want to feature a particular motif, do so on those.

Painted wall surfaces are also cheap and easy to redo. Stencils really

come into their own in a child's room. Be bold and create a theme for the room with motifs that can be repeated on other accessories, bedspreads, and toys. Farm animals suit both boys and girls, as do circuses, underwater themes, or maybe a zoo. Try to keep the colors you use to a fairly limited palette— two main shades, such as red and yellow and an accent color such as blue or green, work best— then you can extend these same colors onto the woodwork too.

If you want to create something truly unique, you could try copying a fun design onto a wall as a painted mural. Use an overhead projector to magnify an image onto the wall while you trace its outline—unless of course you have the flair and confidence to produce something special with a flick of a brush. When your child grows up and wants something more sophisticated it should only take a few hours to repaint in more subtle tones.

To be practical, it is best to choose a scheme that can be easily adapted as your baby grows up and develops strong preferences of his or her own.

Mix and match vibrant colors to make a room fun, bright, and child-friendly.

hall walls

The hallway is the first area of your home that visitors will see, so if you believe that first impressions count, you'll want to make this space as warm and welcoming as you can.

When choosing a color scheme, bear in mind the amount and kind of light the room receives. Many hallways, especially in townhouses, receive very little natural light, in which case you may need to simply accept that it will need to be artificially lit. Trying to create an impression of light with pale walls may simply end up looking dingy. Warm-colored walls, such as golden yellow, look particularly lovely under good lighting (try recessed halogen spotlights) or natural sunlight.

In a hall you need a practical wall surface, as it is bound to suffer more than its fair share of knocks and scrapes—especially if you have children around. You can approach the issue of practicality in two ways. You could opt for a cheap painted surface and accept that it will need to be touched up regularly and repainted every few years. The alternative approach is to choose a surface that is more able to withstand a bump or two. In a traditional

Hall walls need to be welcoming; you can use them to introduce a color theme you can enjoy throughout the whole house.

The natural light flooding into the upper part of this hallway lifts the entire space so it is not too gloomy. Choose lighting carefully if your hall has little or no natural light.

house consider dividing the hall walls with a chair rail at hip height, which will allow you to choose a more expensive paper or finish above it, and a simple paint finish below which can be touched up.

Or cover the lower half of the wall with wooden tongue-and-groove paneling, varnished or painted with an oil-based paint for protection. Even modern homes can look great with wood-paneled walls in the hallway.

The striking color in this hallway adds to the dramatic look of this staircase with its elaborate banister.

hall floors

A wood floor can be buffed and polished to show the natural grain and color of the wood to best effect.

Hall floors need to be durable, but you also want them to be attractive. Choose a flooring which will keep its good looks as years go by.

Hall floors are the perfect place to use bold and decorative designs—as long as you choose a floor surface that is practical too. Bear in mind that the hallway and front door open on to the world outside and, as such, it is inevitable that what is outside will also be carried inside. Leaves, grit, dirt, and dust are all unwelcome, but unavoidable, and your floor surface will need to withstand them.

It is for this reason that many people eschew expensive carpeting in favor of more washable or sweepable surfaces, such as encaustic or natural stone tiles, or wooden flooring. But practical certainly needn't mean dull. Refer to the sections on wood and tiles to see the wide range of attractive materials that are available.

The key to creating a beautiful hall floor, rather than just a satisfactory one, lies in your own confidence. The best hall floors make good use of color or pattern to create an eye-catching space. The hall is the best area in the house in which to make use of bold finishes, as not only is it the first (and sometimes only) part of your home that visitors see, it is also a place where

Encaustic floor tiles are a natural and beautiful choice for a period townhouse.

natural stone tiles

people are always on the move. In a room used for relaxing, eating, or even sleeping, a dramatic floor can be overstimulating and overwhelming, but in the hall it can look fantastic.

Natural stone flooring creates a solid, country-house style.

Take your inspiration from the style of the house and the size of the hallway, but consider, for example, how you might make patterns with beautiful polished woodblock, re-create a stunning Victorian townhouse-style entrance hall with encaustic tiles, or emulate a country manor with oversized flagstones. Whatever you choose, you'll be sure of making a grand entrance.

patterned tile

plain ceramic tile

glass block

bathroom tiles and glass

The colored bathroom suite has fallen out of fashion in the last decade and for many people, white porcelain is now a must. However, you don't want the bathroom to feel cold and clinical, so use the wall space and tiles to inject a bit of color, pattern, and interest into the room.

Old meets new in bathrooms everywhere so don't be afraid to mix glass blocks with mahogany surfaces, or mosaic patterns with Victoriana.

For a traditional effect nothing is better than white tiling, especially if it is laid in a staggered brick-like fashion and topped with a colored edging tile. You can reinforce a historical look with one of the

Tiles and glass will add pattern and color to what might otherwise be a rather clinical space.

many reproduction tile designs. Some tile manufacturers that were producing tiles in the early 20th century are still in business and relaunching some classic designs.

Modern bathrooms also suit a combination of white tiling with a few colored tiles as a feature. Create your own interest with simple patterns or colored tiles, rather than choosing fussy floral designs.

Glass blocks work well if you want to create a divide, perhaps between a shower or toilet and the rest of the bathroom, without losing the impression of space or restricting the light.

White brick-style tiles are the ideal finish for a room where old meets new.

The cool blue walls and white porcelain give a crisp, fresh look to this bathroom.

confidence

Half the battle with interior design is having the confidence to mix and match your surfaces, finishes, furniture, and upholstery effectively. Most manufacturers now provide samples to help you make choices, but ultimately the finished room must appeal to you. Most people want their home to express their personality, so why follow the crowd?

index

list of suppliers

PLASTER

KDS SPECIALTY SERVICES
(800) 390-1637
9436 Fairfield Drive
Twinsburg, OH 44087
www.drywalltextures.com

OPERATIVES PLASTERERS AND
CEMENT MASONS
(301) 470-4200

PAINT & PAINT EFFECTS

BENJAMIN MOORE
(800) 826-2623
www.benjaminmoore.com

THE FAUX MEISTER
148 Carpenter Street
P.O. Box 533
Dushore, PA 18614
Paints, mediums, pigments, brushes, tools

O-GEE PAINT
(888) 385-9969
www.o-geepaint.com
*Faux finishing paints and supplies, including
McCloskey glazes*

OLD FASHIONED MILK PAINT CO.
(978) 448-6336
436 Main Street
P.O. Box 222
Groton, MA 01450
www.milkpaint.com
Colors and effects

THOMPSONS AND FORMBY
(800) 367-6297
825 Crossover Lane
Memphis, TN 38117
Exterior and interior stains

TILES

BEDROSIANS
(559) 275-5000; call for other locations
4285 N. Golden State Boulevard
Fresno, CA 93722
www.bedrosians.com

CENTURY TILE
(630) 889-0800
747 East Roosevelt Road
Lombard, IL 60148
Ceramic and vinyl tile; also various flooring

EDELMAN LEATHERS
(212) 751-3339
Leather floor tiles

FLOORING

ABC CARPET & HOME
(212) 473-3000
888 Broadway
New York, NY 10003

ARMSTRONG WORLD INDUSTRIES
(800) 233-3823
P.O. Box 3001
Lancaster, PA 17604
www.armstrong.com

list of suppliers

CAROUSEL CARPET MILLS
(707) 485-0333
Natural sisal, coir, and jute floorings

PARIS CERAMICS
(212) 644-2784
Stone flooring

PERGO
(800) 33-PERGO
www.pergo.com
Laminate flooring

WOOD FLOORING
INTERNATIONAL
(215) 333-6511; call for distributors
7910-C State Road
Philadelphia, PA 19136
www.wflooring.com

WALLPAPER
LAURA ASHLEY
www.laura-ashleyusa.com
Traditional wallpapers, paints, and paint effects

DESIGNERS GUILD
Available through Osborne & Little
203-359-1500
Stylish wallpapers and paints

AMERICAN BLIND AND WALLPAPER
FACTORY
800-575-9012
www.abwf.com
A selection of mid-range wallcoverings

GLASS AND METAL
BAGGOT LEAF COMPANY
(212) 431-GOLD
430 Broome Street
New York, NY 10013
Catalog of gold- and metal-leafing supplies

S.A. BENDHEIM COMPANY
(212) 226-6370
122 Hudson Street
New York, NY 10013
Hand-blown window glass, art and architectural glass

CHRISTOPHER BRANDNER
DESIGN SOLUTIONS
(732) 224-8692
51 Silverbrook Road
Shrewsbury, NJ 07702
Custom furnishings in wrought iron, cast metal, glass, and wood

HYGRADE POLISHING AND
PLATING CO.
(718) 392-4082
2207 41st Avenue
Long Island City, NY 11101
Metal plating and refinishing

SCHWARTZ'S FORGE
AND METALWORKS
(315) 841-4477
2695 Route 315
Deansboro, NY 13328
Custom architectural metalwork

acknowledgments

The publisher would like to thank the following for their generous assistance with props and photography:

Calvey Taylor-Haw for photography
Lorraine Harrison for proping
Paul Allen for setting up and carrying out the projects;
Sussex Wall & Floor Tiling Ltd., Hove;
King's Framers, Lewes;
Bright Ideas, Lewes;
Mark Jamieson.

Picture credits
Every effort has been made to trace copyright holders and obtain permission. The publishers apologise for any ommissions and would be pleased to make any necessary changes at subsequent printings.

Abode 6br & 40br, 7 & 127, 8t, 10tl, 12b, 14t, 16b, 18b, 19t, 25t, 25b, 27t, 27b, 39t, 40br, 45t, 48b, 49b, 50b, 51t, 51b, 61t, 62b, 67b, 69t, 70b, 91t, 92b, 93t, 106b, 112b, 114b, 117t, 127, 128b, 132b, 133t, 134b, 135, 136b, 137t, 138b, 139t, 140t, 140b, 141t, 141b, 150t, 151t, 157t, 159t, 163tr, 164b, 165b, 174t, 175t, 175b, 178b, 180t, 180b, 181b, 183b, 184bl, 184br, 191t, 193t, 195t, 195b, 196t, 196b, 197, 199b, 200b, 201t, 201b;

The Amtico Company 103t, 115b, 190b, 191b, 198t;

Ceramics of Distinction 104b, 105b, 105t, 108b, 109b;

Corbis / Michael Boys 71b / Tommy Chandler-EWA 46t / Rodney Hyett-EWA 154b;

Dulux 6bl, 15c, 20b, 21b, 24c;

Fired Earth 107t;

Graham & Brown 82b, 83t, 83b;

Harlequin 80b, 86b, 87t, 88b, 89t, 177t, 179t, 185, 186b, 192b;

House & Interiors 14b, 38b, 65t / Roger Brooks 63t, 113t, 128t, 153t, 161b, 194b, 198b / Simon Butcher 23t, 36b, 176b / Ed Buziak 126b / Chris M. Evans 156b, 176t, 181t / Jake Fitzjones 42tl, 152b, 153b, 161t, 163b, 165t / Michael Harris 117t, 187b / Steve Hawkins 49t, 84b, 91b, 150b, 157b, 178t / Nick Higgins 24b, 37tl, 187t / David Markham 183t / Gwennan Murphy 71t / Steve Sparrow 90b / Verne 17t, 43b, 66b, 68b, 85, 155b, 182, 193b;

Ikea 8b, 131b;

Metal Kitsch 9b, 158, 163tl;

Ocean 160b;

Original Style 102b, 110b, 111t, 115t, 199tl;

Sanderson 89b;

Mark Wilkinson Furniture 174b, 188b;

Zoffany 26b, 81t.